BRITAIN IN OLD PHOTOGRAPHS

AXMOUTH
VILLAGE

TED GOSLING & MICHAEL CLEMENT

First published 2008
Reprinted 2014

The History Press
The Mill, Brimscombe Port,
Stroud, Gloucestershire, GL5 2QG
www.thehistorypress.co.uk

Copyright © Ted Gosling & Michael Clement, 2008

Title page photograph: The atmosphere of a Victorian village is apparent in this 1875 photograph of Axmouth.

British Library Cataloguing in Publication Data
A catalogue record for this book is available from the British Library.

ISBN 978-0-7509-4967-5

Typeset in 10.5/13.5 Photina.
Typesetting and origination by The History Press.
Printed and bound in England.

Dedicated to all the people of Axmouth

The Sweetland family, *c.* 1963.

Contents

	Foreword	5
1.	The Village	7
2.	Village People	25
3.	Axmouth Football	63
4.	Schooldays	81
5.	Stedcombe	91
6.	The Axmouth Flood	103
7.	High Days & Events	107
8.	The River Axe & the Harbour	133
	Acknowledgements	160

Axmouth Harbour, 1925.

St Michael's Church Sunday School outing, *c.* 1954.

FOREWORD

Axmouth was once a town of considerable importance in the West Country with its ancient port, used by the Phoenicians. It has even been claimed that Jesus himself, accompanying his uncle, Joseph of Arimethia, landed here en route to Glastonbury. The Romans also landed at Axmouth and established a military base here in AD 49. In the centuries before the shingle bank appeared, it was much used commercially because of its strong transport links; the Fosse Way terminating at Axmouth and a branch of the Icknield Way passing across the River Axe by Boshill.

The Iron Age hillfort of Hawksdown above the village was part of a line of forts built by the Durotriges tribe from Dorset to mark their boundary with Dumnonia. In AD 614 the invading Saxons fought the Battle of Bindon on the site of the old manor above the present village. Following their victory they established the first church, which was later rebuilt by the Normans in about 1140.

Owing to its importance, Axmouth was a Royal Manor belonging to the Saxon kings until it was given to Richard de Redvers, Earl of Devon, during the reign of Henry II. He granted it to the Benedictine Abbey of Montebourg in Normandy. After the suppression of the abbeys by Henry VIII it was given to Queen Catherine Parr as part of her dowry. The manor later passed to the Erle family by marriage to the heiress of the Wykes of Bindon. It was Sir Walter Erle, a Parliamentary General in the Civil War, who undertook the rebuilding of Axmouth Harbour. After Bindon ceased to be a manor house, it was replaced by Stedcombe House in the late eighteenth century when the present Stedcombe was rebuilt after having been burned down in the Civil War.

In 1809 John Hathersall Hallett of Stedcombe continued rebuilding the harbour as we know it today. A long pier, 250ft in length, jutted out into the sea and a customs house with warehouses were erected at the mouth of the river, but later washed away in January 1915. The harbour traded successfully until the arrival of the railway in 1868 when the earliest surviving concrete bridge at Axmouth was built.

It was in Axmouth that the famous landslip took place on Christmas Day, 1839. Two cottages were destroyed and a huge chasm, 300ft wide and nearly a mile long, was created. Queen Victoria even came to inspect it in a paddle-steamer. I remember the Landslip Cottage occupied by old Mrs Gapper, which was renowned for its cream teas.

Axmouth was a tremendously hospitable place and in its heyday was said to have boasted fourteen inns, though sadly only two remain today. Tradition has it that cider was first made in Axmouth by monks; the tradition is still upheld to this day.

This book is a worthy addition to the 'Britain in Old Photographs' series. Ted Gosling, this time with the invaluable assistance of Mike Clement, has created a wonderful record of photographs illustrating the history of Axmouth. It is not before time that Axmouth's story has been told, and it now takes its place as one of the most interesting and historic places in East Devon.

Roy F. Chapple, Chairman of the Axe Valley Heritage Association

There is an atmosphere of unhurried activity in this photograph of Axmouth taken in 1954.

The late Sir John Loveridge and Lady Loveridge stand together outside Bindon. Bindon has been a farmhouse as far back as we know, and it continues to be so.

1

The Village

The gateway to Axmouth, 2004.

Axmouth village, *c.* 1960. In Roman times Axmouth was a significant port. A branch of the Fosse Way ended at Axmouth and the Icknield Way running from Dorchester to Exeter followed an even older trade route. Axmouth was a Roman station called Uxelis and nearby Seaton claims to be the ancient Roman town of Moridunum. In AD 49 Vespasian's 2nd Legion established a military base at Seaton to further his conquest of the west and the siege of Exeter. A legionary title has been found on the Honeyditches Roman villa site. Another Roman villa was located at Holcombe, near Uplyme, and it was the Romans who started mining the stone at Beer Quarries, which was exported by sea from the harbour at Axmouth.

The view from the junction of Bushes Lane and Green Lane, 2005.

St Michael's Church, c. 1955.

Haven Cottage, c. 1890. This thatched cottage on the corner of Kemps Lane was used by the farm workers of Haven Farm.

St Michael's Church, c. 1953. The thatched cottages on the right have unfortunately been demolished and replaced with a more modern building.

Axmouth village, c. 1956. It is sad to think that the cottages on the right have been replaced with a modern building. In the early days, the use of local materials was a distinctive feature of East Devon villages, and in cottages like this you could find charm and nostalgia knowing that these were once the homes of village ancestors.

The atmosphere of Victorian Axmouth is apparent in this 1893 photograph. Devon villages were still independent communities at that time, and in some cases were like colonies shut off from the outside world. The man and little girl standing outside the Harbour Inn were part of a village scene now long gone, where the squire, Sanders Stephens Esq. from Stedcombe Manor, still ruled and made sure that his tenants were in church on Sunday.

The secret charm of the old village life that we so often dream about is reflected in this photograph of Axmouth, taken in 1901.

Axmouth village, *c.* 1954. When we now look at this scene from over fifty years ago, we recognise its beauty and our loss. In this peaceful picture we sense that something we once had has slipped from us, and no apparent gain is compensation. The photograph becomes a token of the gap between now and then.

Mary Broom's working farmhouse kitchen fireplace, *c.* 1959. Mary Broom farmed in Axmouth, and above her mantelpiece is a rack for the long spits used over wood fires. The floor has its original paving of irregularly shaped pieces of flat stone and, although not seen in this photograph, I expect that somewhere was hanging a brass and copper warming pan. In the East Devon farmhouse the principal room was the kitchen, the main features of which were the stone-flagged floor and the capacious fireplace with a cosy inglenook. In the past, unmarried farm labourers lived and boarded at the farm, so the kitchen table, made of oak, was of a size sufficient to seat over a dozen people. Standing against the wall would be huge oak dressers, which would be used to display an assortment of china on their shelves, including with dishes, platters and bowls. Working farmhouse kitchens were the centre of all household activities, and it is rare to find an unspoilt example today.

Axmouth Church, August 1875.
In the towns and villages of East
Devon, the churches with their
towers that dominate the skyline are
often the oldest surviving buildings.
It was during the twelfth century
that a vast building programme
of churches, both large and small,
took place, and from that time they
became the centre of communal life,
giving spiritual comfort to those in
need. The sixteenth century saw the
introduction of parish registers to
record births, baptisms, marriages
and deaths in the community. These
registers, together with the plaques
and tombstones, give a valuable
social history of the village. This
photograph shows the Church of
St Michael at Axmouth. Parts of
the present structure date from the
twelfth century.

The still unspoilt village of Axmouth
and the marshes of the River Axe can
be seen in this photograph, c. 1955.

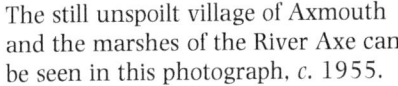

Axmouth village, *c.* 1890. There is something cosy about a thatched roof. It seems to wrap around a house like a blanket, and speaks of warmth and comfort. There could not be a better example of an old Devon thatched cottage than the one pictured here. The chimneys on the cottage are typical of Devonshire houses – great square things, un-ornamented except for a course of bricks around the top, almost like small factory chimneys.

Taken in the 1950s or '60s, this photograph shows nos 47 (nearest) and 48 Church Street and Victoria House. No. 47 was occupied by Bill and Elsie Gapper at this time. Bill was the village shoe repairer and his shop window can be seen to the right of the front door. The entrance to the shop was through the gateway just visible on the extreme right of the photograph.

Axmouth village, *c.* 1956.

A fine view of Axmouth Church and the village, *c.* 1899.

The Ship Inn, February 1966.

The Harbour Inn, February 1966.

Axmouth village, August 1877. Today's village bears little resemblance to the self-contained community it was in Victorian days.

Taken during the summer of 1956, this photograph gives a view of the traditional countryside of the Axe Valley, with its chequerboard of green fields divided by lush hedgerows. The still unspoilt village of Axmouth, with the square tower of the Church of St Michael, can be seen in the centre with the marshes of the River Axe beyond.

Axmouth, *c.* 1884. Life has changed dramatically since the day an unknown photographer took this shot of the village. This was still an age when country people living in the villages of East Devon lived a restricted rural life, geared to the slow rhythm of the changing seasons.

A step back in time, at the bottom of Stepps Lane, *c.* 1895. Stepps House can be seen on the right, and 19 Stepps Lane on the left. The present day name for 19 Stepps Lane is Lattenbells.

The view from Higher Barn field, looking down on Southcombe, Chapel Street and Church Street, August 2005.

Bindon Manor, the home of the late Sir John and Lady Loveridge, August 2005. The manor, like many early houses, has a history which goes back further than we can be certain of, but the walls of the central block on the house have been verified as being twelfth-century. It is thought that at this time it was a small castle which would have been fortified in some way. Bindon is probably one of the oldest sites of which we have knowledge. Roman coins dating from AD 49 have been found near here, but 1,500 years before the Romans came there were agricultural settlements nearby. The old Iron Age fort of Hawkesdown, visible across the valley, was occupied by cattle-farming people who lived here about two hundred years BC.

A unique picture of Higher Axmouth, *c.* 1900. Here we can see the old cottage on the right, which stood by the lane up to Spring Cottage. This cottage, built of traditional Devon cob, collapsed in the 1950s owing, no doubt, to poor maintenance.

The farmyard at Coombe Farm, *c.* 1901. This was still an age when real country people lived in the village, and the vast number of agricultural labourers were the biggest class in East Devon.

A peaceful scene in Church Street, c. 1985.

Stepps House, c. 1958. This fifteenth-century building was once a mansion of considerable proportion and was the home of the Mallock family until they moved to Rousdon in about 1617. Subsequently, it was converted into five small cottages, during which time much of its medieval character was obliterated. Happily not entirely so, for during its restoration in 1931 many of its most attractive features were discovered. At the time of this picture Stepps was a small hotel and country club.

The Old Forge, Axmouth, *c.* 2005.

The view from the field above Haven Farm, looking down on Coldwell Lane, Kemps Lane, the old vicarage and part of Pound Hill, July 2004.

The Gospel Hall Chapel, c. 1900. The Plymouth Brethren, an austere Protestant sect founded in Plymouth in 1830 by a former Anglican priest, J.N. Darby (1800–82), had strict standards of behaviour. At one time they had small chapels in most East Devon villages, and the chapel in Axmouth was officially opened on Friday 26 August 1864. For nearly 100 years this Gospel Hall was well supported. It might well be that chapels like this were the creed of a working class minority who refused to accept the dominance of the establishment and the old village squire. Sadly the congregation declined, and the last service held in the hall was for Elsie Gapper, one of the last Gospel Hall village elders, who died on 6 September 1987. The chapel was then sold, and is now a private house.

The old natives of Axmouth used to say that the water piped down from Spring Head was the purest in the country. This must have been after 1883, because before that date the water used in the village was dipped from the brook. Even then the only water in the village that was pure came from the water fountain, which was given by William T. Hallett Esq. of Stedcombe. This picture, taken in 2005 in the bus stop opposite the Ship Inn, shows all that remains of the fountain.

Chapel Street looking down from Southcombe Farm. The old post office is on the left-hand side and the chapel is lower down on the right. Before the chapel was built and opened in 1864, this street was known as Broad Street.

Higher Axmouth at the end of the nineteenth century.

2

Village People

Axmouth Home Guard, c. 1942. The plan to raise Local Defence Volunteers in 1940 met with an immediate response in East Devon. The name was soon changed to the Home Guard, although they were known affectionately as 'Dad's Army'. By the end of 1940 the Home Guard numbered 1.5 million men nationally and during the preparations for D-Day in 1944 they took over most of the security duties on the Home Front. The men from the village of Axmouth played an important part in the Second World War, and after their final muster in 1945 the community expressed immense gratitude to them for all the voluntary work they had done during the difficult time of war. Back row, left to right: Jeff Puddicombe, Gordon Hunt, Ray Hunt, Leslie Hunt, Mr Mann Snr, Mr Mann Jnr. Middle row: Herbie Clements, Jack Good, Ted Snell, Jim Cross, Jim Board, Ken Morgan, Mr Mann. Front row: Frank Snell, Harry Newbery, Len Weekes, the Revd Swift, Howie Owen, Ken Webber, Victor Worden.

William (Bill) Rice, with horse and putt, near Coombe Farm, October 1931. Bill Rice had the contract from Devon County Council for cleaning the brook running through the village. This picture shows his daughter Ada sitting in the putt, which was made by Henry Crichard of Axmouth at a cost of £15. Henry Crichard also made coffins for the village and his old cottage and workshop used to be below the Harbour Inn, where Little Thatch now stands. Bill Rice's horse, Jip, served with the British Army, and was stamped with the army brand. Jip died at the ripe old age of thirty-five.

Outside the Ship Inn, Axmouth, 1930s. Four brothers home on leave from the armed services. Left to right: Stanley Morgan (Royal Navy), Tom Morgan (Royal Navy), Herbert Morgan (Royal Marines), Jack Morgan (Royal Marines).

'Dads Army' ready for action – Axmouth Local Defence Volunteers, the forerunners of the Home Guard, were formed in about 1940. Left to right: Wilfred Rice, Percy Clement, Jim Cross, -?-, Ernie Tucker, George (Biddy) Morgan, Ambrose Spiller, the Revd Henry Meade Swifte, Harry Newbery, Henry Snell, with Reg Morgan behind.

This picture shows Seaton in the 1960s with, left to right: Walter Newbery from Axmouth, Wilfred Hutchings from Seaton, Philip Soper and Ronald Beasley from Axmouth.

The Ship Inn, Axmouth, c. 1935. The landlord of the Ship Inn from 1926 until 1953 was William Worden, pictured here with family members outside the pub. Left to right: Miss Peggy Worden, Mr Eric Worden, Mrs W. Worden (landlady), Miss Eileen Worden, Mr William Worden and Douglas Worden. William was a big-boned giant of a man. An ex-policeman, he would settle any trouble in his pub by picking up the culprit and throwing him into the nearby brook. An important job he undertook in the village was the butchering of pigs. Before the Second World War most village people kept a pig, and Worden butchered them in the skittle alley of his pub. They always squealed when William arrived wearing his apron, with a little sticking knife in his hand. They would do everything to evade capture, but to no avail.

The Ship Inn 'B' Darts Team of the Seaton Darts League outside the pub, c. 1954. Back row, left to right: Ted Board, Eric Childs (landlord), John Purse. Front row: David Vaughan, Herbie Clement, Raymond Gush, Freda Childs, Bill Busby.

In 1950 June Sweetland was the Queen Attendant at Axmouth Flower Show, and she is pictured here on the Queen's float. To her left is her sister Amy, who was also one of the attendants.

Seaton garage owner Mr Ben Trevett is seen taking his daughter to Axmouth church on her wedding day, summer 1919.

Jack Widger and family, Seaton beach, c. 1959. Jack Widger, from Axmouth, had the beach hut and deckchair concession from the SUDC. He was a much-loved man, and was well-known to thousands of holiday makers. He is pictured here as so many will remember him. Left to right: Una Board, May Widger, Jack Widger (in the beach hut), Ernest Widger, John Widger, Betty Widger (Jack's wife), Geoffrey Richards, June Richards.

Smiles were the order of the day in this photograph of the Sweetland and Widger families on Seaton beach during the summer of 1963.

The Sweetland family of Axmouth, *c.* 1934. Left to right, back row: Betty (holding June), Eunice and Amy. Front: John and Peter.

The Dack family at Stepps Lane, Axmouth, c. 1944. From back, left to right: Ross, Patricia, Keith, father Hugh (holding Maxwell), Bruce.

Harbour Inn, early 1960s. Seated around the table skittles board are, left to right: Roy Beasley, Les Harvey, Herbert Clement, Albert Soper, Edward Soper and Charlie Male.

William Newbery in his Sunday best at Axmouth, just after the First World War.

Three village characters outside the old village shop (later the post office), 1950s. Reginald Morgan, from Coombe Terrace (with bicycle) lost an eye in the First World War, while serving in the Royal Navy, and he lost one of his sons during the Second World War.
The other two are Percival Real, who lived next door to the shop (now Blossom Cottage), and Tom Spiller from Southcombe Terrace.

Gerald and Miriam Legg with their son Robin at Elm Orchard, Axmouth, 1958. Gerald worked on village farms for many years before getting involved in building work.

The Golden Wedding celebrations of Laura and Percival Clement, Knapp House, 26 December 1960. Laura and Percival lived at Knapp House from 1928 until their deaths in 1972 and 1974 respectively.

1st Axmouth Brownies, in Axmouth churchyard, waiting to form a guard of honour at the wedding of June Sweetland and Roderick Richards, *c.* 1952. Left to right: Gwen Ostler, Joy Hansford, Pauline Real, Barbara Spiller, Shirley Newbery, Jeannie Johns. (See also pp. 60–1)

1st Axmouth Brownies in the old football field (now the camp site), *c.* 1950. Joy Hansford, Gwen Shepherd, Pauline Real and Brown Owl Margaret Northcott.

Herbie and Michael Sweetland, 1949.

Chapel Street, with Sunnyhayes and the Gospel Hall in the background, 13 August 1949. Left to right: Douglas Spiller, Herbie Sweetland, Peter Sweetland, John Sweetland and Michael Sweetland.

A group of young people from Axmouth watch the Couchill Scramble, Seaton, 1956. Left to right: Fred Vaughan, Raymond Vaughan, Celia Morgan, Michael Pidgeon and Michael Sweetland.

This photograph of Michael Sweetland, seen here on 4 August 1957, is a sad reminder of the tragic accidents that affected Axmouth and left three families in mourning. Two days after this picture was taken Michael, then only sixteen years old, was killed in a motorcycle accident. Just eighteen days after this sad event another Axmouth boy, sixteen-year-old Alan Johns, was also killed in a motorcycle crash. This was followed a few months later by the death of another young boy, Donald Ostler, who was also killed in a similar accident.

Chapel Street, c. 1934. Views of people and streets like this bring long-gone days back to life. Rose Real and Alice Larcombe are pictured feeding the ducks that once lived and swam in Axmouth brook. At that time the brook was open and flowed down through the village.

Cousins Robin Legg (left) and Keith Legg take it easy sitting on the new seat at Coronation Corner, c. 1954.

Mr and Mrs C. Sweetland, pictured on 13 August 1944. The family moved from 7 Higher Axmouth to Sunnyhayes in Chapel Street in 1944. At Sunnyhayes Charlie reared pigs, chickens and geese. He also had a large garden where produce and flowers were grown and sold to the folk of the village. Winifred, his wife, acted as the village midwife. For many years she washed and also carried out necessary repairs to the kit of the village football team. She was also involved, along with many other village ladies, in dance classes, village social evenings, the Village Produce Association, whist drives, jumble sales, the village children's Christmas parties and the bingo.

Jack Beer, a well-known Axmouth character, sitting in his favourite seat in the Harbour Inn, c. 1955.

Ludovic Grant, Axmouth, c. 1956. Ludovic was mine host at the Harbour Inn between 1950 and 1958. He took over the licence from the Beer family, who had been landlords for the previous eighty years. Ludo, or 'Mr G.' as he was known, renovated and restored the Harbour. He made an extra bar, the Inner Bar, in the old bowling alley at the rear. He was a great showman and a well-loved local character. In the days when pubs didn't serve food apart from sandwiches and crisps, hundreds of hot pasties, which came from a Seaton baker, were sold at the Harbour during the summer months. Mr G. bought Miss Sanders Stephens' 1923 Rolls-Royce, which was used as an attraction and stood in the car park for several years, until he discovered it was being used as overnight accommodation.

The Harbour Inn staff, mid-1960s. Left to right, back row: Charlie Chapple, Annie Humphrey, Philip Sober, Herbie Clement, Albert Soper, Dorothy Rodmore (landlady), Marcus Rodmore (landlord), Percy Clement, Philip Badcock, Rodney Boyce, Ron Beasley. Front row: Henry Clement, Florence Clement, -?-, Emma Johns, Linda Pike, Maureen Humphrey, Betty Hoare, Jack Shepherd.

Mariah Ayres, Alice Tipper and her daughter Miriam at Pound Hill, Axmouth, *c.* 1923.

Roy (Duke) Beasley and Bill Busby at Seaton Club, *c.* 1953. Bill now lives at Honiton. Roy, who was always the life and soul of anything he took part in (football, darts, skittles or card games) died suddenly at the age of fifty-seven in 1995. His death was a huge loss to everyone who knew him and the church at Axmouth was packed for his funeral.

The yawning gap between our age today and the past is reflected in this family photograph of the Morgans, *c.* 1922. Left to right, back: Tom Morgan, Jack Morgan. Front: Leslie Harvey, Herbert Morgan and Queenie Morgan.

The workers of Coombe Farm pose for this photograph, which was taken in a field between Higher Barn Lane and Spring Cottage, *c.* 1955. Left to right: Albert Soper, Tony Widger, Neil MacDermid and George Haynes.

Farrier-Staff Sergeant Major Oliver Thomas Spiller, Royal Horse Artillery, and his wife Florence. Oliver (Tom) Spiller served for twenty-two years in the army, and was awarded the Croix-de-Guerre for bravery in the First World War.

Harry Beasley at his home at Pound Hill, 1940s. Harry was a great supporter of the village football team. The house where he lived is now known as Curlews.

Lewis Price, also known as Sam, gentleman of the road. This photograph was taken at the piece of wasteground at the bottom of Stepps Lane, now the site of Stepps Cross Cottage. Lewis was at Axmouth for many years, using the village post office for his pension, and both village inns for a drink. He had a mate who came on a bicycle to visit him every year, who was an old-fashioned knife-sharpener. Here Lewis is sitting beside his fire, with the smoke drifting all around. He lived to the grand old age of ninety-two, passing away in 1994, and is buried in Axmouth churchyard.

Herbert Clement Snr at his home at Coombe Orchard, Axmouth, 1969. Herbert worked for many years as a steamroller driver for Devon County Council. He served with the Devonshire Regiment in the First World War where he saw heavy action in the retreat from Mons, for his part in this he was awarded the Mons Star. He was a dab hand at catching rabbits with ferret and nets. He loved to play table skittles at the Harbour Inn, with a pint of cider for the winner. He was never without his pipe. His latter years saw him working at Warners Holiday Camp, Seaton. Herbert passed away in 1970, aged seventy-six. He was certainly one of the village characters.

Seaton West Walk, *c.* 1967. Axmouth lads Ron Real (left) and Mike Clement, who was home on leave from the Merchant Navy.

Thomas John Morgan (Jack) was born in Salcombe Regis and came to Axmouth as a baby. He is pictured here on his wedding day in 1931, with his wife Florena. The lady to his right with the lace collar, was Granny Morgan, the family matriarch. During the Second World War Jack served with 45 Marine Commando and saw action on D-Day. He also fought in France, Holland and Belgium. He left the Royal Marines in 1946 with the rank of lieutenant after twenty-two years' service.

Frederick Carl Jarchow (1911–85). Always known as Jack, Jarchow taught Classic English Literature at Allhallows School, Rousdon, and in his later years was bursar at the school. Jack was a great character and lived with his wife, Betty, in the Toll House at Axmouth Bridge. He drove a green MG sports car, and was known for his passion for cricket. During the Second World War he saw active service in Italy, Crete and Sicily. When asked what were his main interests in life he would always reply 'C.C.C.', which stood for classics, cricket and consuming. Jack loved to frequent the Harbour Inn for his pint of scrumpy, which would always be followed with a pinch of snuff.

Stepps Country Club, early 1980s. Left to right: Ned Spiller, Nora Myers, Graham Myers, Mark Northcott, Pat Trezise.

Freda Myers with the family cat, Ben, in the garden at Haven Cottage, 1970s.

Stepps Country Club, early 1980s. Left to right: Ned Spiller, Mark Northcott, Barry and Lesley Saxby.

Coldwell Lane, July 2005. Alex Hunt (left) and Jared Steven having a kick around in the back yard.

Pictured at the bottom of Coldwell Lane on 1 July 2005 are Axmouth boys Seth Wakeley (left) and David Goodhew.

Waiting for the Seaton school bus to arrive, Coldwell Lane, Axmouth, 27 June 2005. Left to right: Nicky Wakeley, Seth Wakeley, Jacob Hale (in pushchair), Paul Snell with Amber and Jack (in pushchair), Jared Steven.

Winter snow at Axmouth, with a sledging party at Hawkesdown Hill, 25 November 2005. They have just completed a run, sitting on an upturned tractor mudguard. Left to right: Callum Elliot, Ben Clinch, Alex Hunt, Jessica Llewellyn, Anna Elliott, James Gabb.

The Squire family at the Harbour Inn, Axmouth. They left the pub after thirty-six years in charge, September 2005. Left to right: Andrew, Paul, David, Patricia and Philip.

Christmas Eve morning, 2005. A group about to set off to cut the Ashen Faggot for the ceremony of Burning the Ashen Faggot at the Harbour Inn on the night of Christmas Eve. Left to right: Brian Davis, David Trezise, Ian Hunt and Mike Calvert.

Trafalgar Day, 21 October 2005. Axmouth celebrated the 200th anniversary of that Battle of Trafalgar with a special dinner, held in the village hall. In this photograph are Christine Badger, Ron Badger, Carol Smith and Wilfred Gribble.

Harold (Bob) and Betty Martin at Stepps Country Club, 1980. Bob Martin (as he was always known) was a retired prison officer at the infamous Dartmoor Prison, and on coming to Axmouth with his wife he took up the post of traffic warden in Seaton and Beer. On one occasion while on duty in Beer, he came face-to-face with one of his former inmates at Dartmoor, a surprise to both of them. Betty was a member of the Village Produce Association, and a regular churchgoer. At one time she was also the Honorary Secretary of Axmouth WI.

Betty Bater, the last postmistress of Axmouth Post Office. The post office closed in July 2001. This photograph was taken at Betty's farewell party in Axmouth Village Hall, before she moved to Cambridgeshire.

Photographed in about 1984, Edward Spiller (left) and Wilfred Rice are true village characters. Edward, always known as Ned, was a keen gardener who served on the flower show committee and also on the Football Club committee. Wilf was also a keen gardener, and had his own haulage business in the village.

The morning delivery, summer 2005. Post lady Linda Baker from Seaton sorting office delivers the mail in Chapel Street.

Betty Board and her dog Casey, Higher Lane, Axmouth, summer 2003.

Minnie Newbery and her nephew, Michael Gush, collecting for the Seaton & District Cancer Fund in Coldwell Lane, 2005.

Tony Widger with his Ferguson tractor, which he rebuilt from scratch at his home in Coombe Orchard. Tony dressed up as Noddy for the Colyton Vintage Tractor Run in 2005.

Pictured here in the 1960s are Axmouth boys Sandy Dack (far left), and Ross Dack (far right) enjoying a night out in Lloret de Mar on the Costa Brava.

Lola Walton, mine hostess at Stepps Country Club, on Burns Night, 25 January 1980.

Axmouth Flower Show, 1993. Peggy Whinfrey and Nora Myers, from Axmouth Women's Institute, providing the teas in the marquee.

Donald Mariner of Stedcombe seated on his 200cc Triumph Tiger Cub, 16 November 2005. Donald served in the Merchant Navy during the Second World War. He came to Axmouth in 1968, with his wife Joyce and their three sons, to work for Sir John Loveridge at Bindon Farm. The family lived in the village for many years and on coming up to his retirement, Donald took up a gardening position at Allhallows School, Rousdon. Donald, Joyce and their youngest son Les, eventually moved to the old farmhouse at Stedcombe.

Mr J. Morrish showing parents a cardboard model of a tank, which was a joint production in the children's handicraft class. Axmouth potter Oliver Moss and his wife Joyce are on the right of this picture.

The ruby wedding celebrations of Phyllis and George Morgan, 2001. Phyllis and Jack Real returned from Canada for the party. Left to right: Phyllis Real, Ethel Clement, Jack Real. They were all neighbours living in Coldwell Lane.

Kemps Lane flats, Axmouth, 1981. On the garden seat are, left to right: Herbie Clement, Annie Humphrey and Alice Larcombe with Wally the dog (who belonged to Barbara and Denny Down).

The marriage of June Sweetland of Axmouth to Roderick Richards of Seaton, *c.* 1952. The 1st Axmouth Brownies form a Guard of Honour at St Michael's Church.

1st Axmouth Brownies at Coombe Farm, *c.* 1957. Left to right: Valerie Soper, Anne Donaldson, Jeanette Spiller, Janet Newbery, Ann Newbery, Carole Hoare and Rusty the dog.

Sarah Ostler serves a young lady with a daily newspaper at the camp site during the summer of 2004.

3

Axmouth Football

Axmouth United AFC, 1986/7 at Stedcombe Mead Ground. They were members of the Perry Street & District Football League, Division 1. Back row, left to right: John Pidgeon, Colin Hales, Dave Harris, Neil Miller, Carl Northcott, Richard Gush, Nick Ostler, John Chaplin (linesman). Front row: Pete Scotchford (Manager), Paul Northcott (Chairman), Peter Northcott, Ashley Wakeley, Geoff Davis, John Widger, Nigel Morgan.

Axmouth United AFC, 1985/6. This was the first time the club had been sponsored for a complete new kit, by R.W. Dack & Sons. Back row, left to right: Mike Clement (Assistant Secretary), Vincent Trevett, Paul Northcott (Chairman), Dave Beardsell, Mark Ward, Nick Ostler, Dave Harris, Graham Wakley, Philip Widger, Gary Millman, Neil Widger, Peter Scotchford (Manager). Front row: Ashley Wakley, John Widger (Captain), Geoff Davis, Peter Northcott, Mark Northcott, Carl Northcott, Andrew Widger (mascot).

Peter Northcott – Axmouth United Player of the Year, season 1983/4. The picture shows Peter Northcott receiving the Michael Sweetland Memorial Trophy from Nancy Sweetland.

Axmouth United AFC, Perry Street League, Intermediate Southern Section, *c.* 1953/4. This photograph was taken in the field behind the Harbour Inn. Back row, left to right: Reg Hoare (linesman), Basil Pavey, Tommy Morgan, Dennis Morgan, David Newbery, Clive Fox, Douglas Lyne, Arthur (Sam) Ayres (Secretary). Front row: Michael Powling, Raymond Gush, Fred Newbery, Ronald Board, Edwin Newbery.

Harbour Inn, November 1985. Pulmans Weekly News reporter John Fletcher (right), presents Axmouth United FC Captain Phil Widger with Pulmans Match Ball, for the 'Team of the Month' for November 1985. They are watched by Gilbert Hutchings (Secretary), Pete Scotchford (Manager), Mike Clement (Assistant Secretary), Geoff Davis and Carl Northcott.

Axmouth United AFC, Perry Street League, Intermediate Southern Section, *c.* 1955/6. This photograph was taken in the field behind the Harbour Inn. Back row, left to right: Arthur Ayres (Secretary), Grenville Morgan, Raymond Gush, David Newbery, Fred Newbery, John Sweetland, Brian Tidball. Front, kneeling: Paul Northcott, Herbie Sweetland, Peter Sweetland, Keith Millman (mascot), Lewis Newbery, Ted Board.

Axmouth AFC, 1925/6. Photographed in the field behind the Harbour Inn, the team colours were blue and white at this time. Back row, left to right: Bernard Nash, Ron Jones, Jack Purton, John Beasley (goalkeeper), Harry Board, Joe Poole, ? English. Front row: Ern Richards, Harold Northcott, Jack Bullock, Oliver Potter.

Presentations at the Axmouth United FC dinner, the Harbour Inn, late 1980s. Left to right: Dean Morgan, Barbara Morgan, Tony Widger, Paul Northcott, John Widger, Pete Scotchford, Norma Sweetland.

Axmouth FC of the Axe Vale Football League/Seaton Hospital Cup Winners, 1935/6. They beat Charmouth 3–0 in the final at Colyford Road, Seaton. The scorers were Arthur Tipper, Douglas Morgan and Douglas Worden. The team colours at that time were claret and sky blue. This picture was taken at the old ground, behind the Harbour Inn. Standing, left to right: G.J. Ayres, J.B. Real, B.A.H. Billows (St John Ambulance), K.H. Webber, A. Somers, J.A. Real, H.L. Morgan, F.C. Dack, H.R. Owen (Secretary), T.E. Tipper, R.W. Morgan, A.E.W. Spiller. Middle row: G.A. Morgan, A.D. Tipper, D.R. Morgan, S.D. Worden, H. Clement, R.J. Cross (kneeling). Front row: E.M. Spiller, G.A.O. Spiller (Captain, holding the Seaton Hospital Cup), A.E. Parker.

Axmouth United AFC of Perry Street League, Division 2. Photographed at Hinton St George during the 1975/6 season, here we see, back row, left to right: John Norman (linesman), Jasper Highet, Adrian Potter, Bob Grimshaw, -?-, John Widger, Nigel Morgan, Dave Evans, Clive Dallimore. Front row: Malcolm MacDonald, Brian Robinson, Pete Scotchford, Gary Millman, Dean Morgan.

Axmouth United AFC was re-formed in 1948, after the Second World War. The club entered the Perry Street League, Intermediate Southern Section in 1949. As the people of the village helped to re-form the club, 'United' was added to its title. Back row, left to right: Gerald Legg, John Collins, Jack Real, Ben Newbery, David Newbery, Arthur Ayres. Front row: Basil Pavey, Ted Board, Herbie Clement, Fred Newbery, Peter Sweetland.

Axmouth United versus Torrington AFC, 1994. This was a fund-raising event at the Musbury Road ground. Among the back row are: Rob Sweetland, Steve Woodman, Alan Potter, Mark Rooke, John Widger, Carl Northcott, Chris Sweetland, Andrew Widger (of Torrington who organised the game), Mike Clement (Chairman, Axmouth FC), John Broom (referee). The front row includes: Glynn Roberts, Richard Gush (linesman), Phil Squire, Dave Mitcham, Geoff Davis, Craig Alexander, Matt Rowson.

Axmouth United AFC, of the Devon & Exeter Football League, Intermediate Division 1, at the Musbury Road ground, 2001/2. Back row, left to right: Mike Clement (Secretary), Dave Turner, James Mills, Mark Holmes, Chris Hammett, James Harvey, Sam Bastin, Mervyn Joslin (Manager). Front row: Keith Kellam, Richard Voysey, Paul Hawkins, Tim Vincent, Shaun Waddon, Dan Reynolds, Phil Squire.

Axmouth United FC dinner at the Pole Arms, Seaton, 1961. Back table, left to right: Roger Searle, David Dack, -?-, Walter Hutchings, Tony Widger, Raymond Vaughan, Stuart Richards, Bernard Webber. Middle table: Georgie Pidgeon, Barbara Down, Dennis Down, Susan Webber, Leslie Legg, Roy Beasley, Barry Clarke, Joan Webber, -?-. Front table: Herbie Sweetland, Norma Sweetland, Amy Purse, John Sweetland, Bruce Dack, Tim Dack, June Richards, John Purse, Helen Sweetland. Top table (far right): Ron Beasley, Emma Hutchings, Gilbert Hutchings (Secretary), Olive Hutchings, Jack Pinn (landlord of the Ship Inn), Arthur Ayres (Chairman), Marcus Rodmore (landlord of the Harbour Inn), and a Perry Street League official.

Axmouth United FC. The opening of the new clubhouse at the Musbury Road ground, 10 August 2002. The opening was performed by Mr Arthur Ayres, a former player, Secretary and Chairman of the club. He is seen here with Mr Gilbert Hutchings, President and former player and Secretary (left), and Mr Edwin Newbery, former player and club Chairman (right).

Much fund-raising was done during the re-formation of the club, 1948/9. A team of ladies played against the men's team in fancy dress on the field behind the Harbour Inn, 1949. Seen here is the ladies' team, in Axmouth United shirts. Back row, left to right: Emma Johns, Betty Widger, Mary Webber, Winifred Maidment, Betty Furzey. Front row: Dinah Millman, Irene Beasley, Eleanor Newbery, Kathleen Ostler, Margaret Northcott, June Sweetland.

More fund-raising activity, with the ladies in fancy dress this time, for a match around the time the club was re-formed, 1949. Back row, left to right: Enid Owen, Gladys Spiller, Hilda Beasley, Dinah Millman, Nell Clement. Front row: May Tucker, Winifred Sweetland, Emma Johns, Mary Webber.

Seen here at the old ground behind the Harbour Inn are three brothers, all playing for Axmouth FC, 1948. Left to right, Ben, Fred and David Newbery.

The official opening of Axmouth United FC's new ground at Musbury Road, Boshill, 14 July 1990. Left to right: Brian Newbery (of the Perry Street & District Football League), Paul Northcott (Chairman of Axmouth United FC) and Cecil Sansom (also of the Perry Street & District Football League).

Axmouth United Ladies Team at the Musbury Road ground, 1996. Back row, left to right: Hannah Fouracre, Chamina Handley, Jo Churchill, Hayley Rosling, Alison Scotchford, Kerry Laxton, Hanna Ingram, Lyn Beavis, Linda Pike, Jo Dibble, Steve Cruwys (Manager). Front row: Erica Farmer, Michelle Cloud, Emma Silvester, Lisa Cowling, Linda Bulpin, Kathy Corrigan, Cheryl Morgan.

Axmouth United AFC photographed at Chard, *c.* 1987. In this season the team were in the Perry Street & District League, Division 2. Back row, left to right: John Chaplin (linesman), Neil Miller, John Pidgeon, Nick Ostler, Alex Sandman, Carl Northcott, Colin Hales. Front row: John Widger, Geoff Davis, Nick Driver, Mark Northcott, Dave Harris.

Musbury Road ground, Axmouth, 2004. Margaret and Don Hansford (left), representing the Devon Air Ambulance, receive a cheque from Ross Dack, Chairman of Axmouth United FC, and Mr Gilbert Hutchings. The money was raised with the Geoff Davis Memorial five-a-side Football Competition.

Axmouth United FC prepare to play boules at their ground against Golden Hind A, in Division 1 of the Axe Valley Boules League, 28 June 2005. Left to right: Paul Tipping, Peter Apps, Colin Small, Liz Tipping, Mark Perry, Ralph Ford.

Axmouth United FC committee members at the Musbury Road Ground, 29 June 2005. Left to right: Keith Kellam (Secretary), Michelle Harvey, James Harvey (Treasurer, holding daughter Isla), Shaun Waddon (Manager), Stephanie Hill, Peter Letten.

Ralph Hay (right) did a sponsored parachute jump at Dunkeswell Aerodrome, 4 August 1987. One of his sponsors was Grenville Morgan (left). In total Ralph raised £261.50 for Axmouth United FC's new ground.

The Axmouth FC players, seen here in August 2004, were one of two Axmouth teams taking part in the Geoff Davis Memorial five-a-side Football Competition. Left to right: Paul Hawkins, Mark Ferreira, James Harvey, Keith Kellam and Sam Bastin.

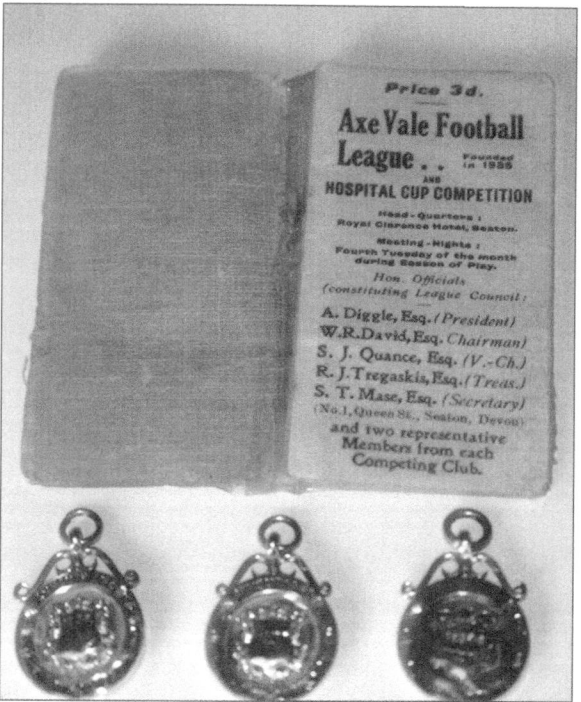

This image is unique to Axmouth FC. It shows the Axe Vale Football League Handbook, price 3d. It belonged to the late Jack Real, who passed away in Canada in 2005. Jack was the Axmouth goalkeeper in all three finals that the club appeared in during the 1930s. Also pictured are the three winning Seaton Hospital Cup Final Medals, for the seasons 1935/6 (when they beat Charmouth), 1936/7 (with victory over Charmouth again), and 1937/8 (when they beat Feniton). These belonged to the late Edward Spiller, who also played in all three finals. Axmouth were the only team in the Axe Vale League ever to win the Seaton, Beer and District Memorial Cottage Hospital Cup, to give it its full title from the handbook. They never lost a game while playing in this competition.

The Axmouth team which played Colyton, 14 September 1935. In the team are, back row, left to right: Joe Poole, Syd Humphrey, Jack Real, Mick Dack, Holway Webber, George Perry (linesman). Front row: Arthur Tipper, John Parker, Geoffrey Spiller, Douglas Morgan, Herbie Morgan, Douglas Webber.

Axmouth United AFC, Perry Street & District Football League, season 1981/2. Back row, left to right: Graham Wakely, John Widger, Peter Northcott, Rob Sweetland, Nick Ostler, Gary Millman, Vincent Trevett, Andy Crichard. Front row: Kevin Grimshaw, Dean Morgan, Mervyn Berry, Mark Northcott, Geoff Davis, Andrew Widger (mascot).

Axmouth United FC, 1968/9, when they were in Division 3 of the Perry Street & District Football League. This photograph was taken in the Village Hall car park in May 1969. The trophies in front of the players are for winning Division 3, the Division 3 Cup and the Tommy Tabberer Cup. Back row, left to right: Mike Clement, Philip Widger, Michael Long, Richard Hales, Melvin Millman, Alan Mitchell, Peter Perryman. Front row: Gerald Morgan, Keith Millman, Malcolm Macdonald, Terry Pavey, Richard Board. Missing from the photograph are other players: Tony Widger, Robin Legg, Peter Scotchford, Rodney Morgan, Keith Legg and Ralph Moore.

Axmouth United FC, 1968/9. The committee with players and trophies in the Village Hall car park in May 1969. Left to right: Edwin Newbery (Chairman), Gilbert Hutchings (Secretary), David Newbery, Philip Widger, Michael Long, Richard Hales, Melvin Millman, Alan Mitchell, Reg Hoare (linesman), Fred Newbery, Walter Hutchings, Jack Morgan (Treasurer). Players: Mike Clement, Gerald Morgan, Keith Millman, Malcolm Macdonald, Terry Pavey, Richard Board, Peter Perryman.

Axmouth United FC at the Pole Arms Hotel for the club dinner in 1962. Far table, left to right: Dennis Down, Barbara Down, Linda Pike, Georgina Pidgeon, Doreen Pavey, Laura Clement, John Sweetland, Helen Sweetland, Norma Sweetland, Herbie Sweetland, Roger Searle, Tim Dack. Middle table: Stuart Richards, Elsie Pavey, Jennie Clarke, Susan Webber, Celia Pavey, Terry Pavey, -?-, Roger Webber, Cedric Slynn, Dianna Slynn, Nancy Sweetland, June Richards. Nearside table: Ted Board, Paul Northcott, Joan Webber, Roy Beasley, Bruce Dack, Jack Emmett, Sheila Board, Frances Northcott, Amy Purse, John Purse, Herbie Bastone. Top table (on far right): Alice Larcombe, David Newbery, Marcus Rodmore, Jack Pinn, Olive Hutchings, Gilbert Hutchings, Edwin Newbery, Barbara Newbery, Victor Muggeridge.

Axmouth United FC at the Pole Arms Hotel for the club dinner in 1962. Nearside table, left to right: Jennie Clarke, Susan Webber, Celia Pavey, Terry Pavey, June Richards, Nancy Sweetland, Dianna Slynn, Cedric Slynn, Roger Webber. Top table: Marcus Rodmore (landlord of the Harbour Inn), Jack Pinn (landlord of the Ship Inn), Olive Hutchings, Gilbert Hutchings, Edwin Newbery, Barbara Newbery, Victor Muggeridge (of the Perry Street & District Football League).

Axmouth United pre-season game at Musbury Road ground, 2005/6. Back row, left to right: Richard Challis, Ed Harrison, Michael Challis, Peter Letten, James Harvey, Stuart French. Front row: Mark Salter, Danny Reynolds, Asa Sandman, Gary Sims, Rob Widger, Chris French.

Axmouth United FC annual dinner at the Wheelwright Inn, Colyford, May 2003. Around the table, left to right: Frances Northcott, Sue Goddard, Chris Hammett, Emma Voysey, Sylvia Voysey, John Voysey, Carl Northcott, Lynn Armstrong, Paul Northcott.

4

Schooldays

Axmouth Village School, 1898. Back row, left to right: Albert England, William England, ? Hawker, Percy Real, Reg Morgan, ? Moulding, Jack Snell, ? Hawker, Edwin Bennett. Middle row: Mrs Gill, Mrs Major (teachers), Nancy Major, Wilfred Real, Daisy Morgan, Clara Snell, Lily Morgan, Meg Snell, Bessie England, Annie England, ? Moulding, Tom Morgan, Gertie Bright, Mr Gill (Headmaster). Front row: Ellie Gill, Arthur Bright, Arthur Morgan, May Real, Henry Crichard, Bessie Crichard, Edie Moulding, Frank Snell, Will Crichard, ? Hawker, Edith Welch, Olive Bright, ? Mitchell, Emma Parsons, ? Jefford, George Morgan, Oliver Morgan, Blanche Spiller.

The village school was always the heart of the community, and the memories of it still linger on with former pupils. There was a school at Axmouth before 1840, which received financial assistance from the estate at Downlands. Its exact position is not known, although it seems highly likely it would have been on the same site as the later school built opposite the Harbour Inn.

A new National School was built at Axmouth on the present site in 1845. The original building consisted of just a schoolroom, and continued in this one room until 1895. The Squire, Samuel Sanders Stephens, then built an extension to accommodate the large number of children in the village at that time.

It continued to have a senior school until 1945, when pupils over the age of eleven transferred to either Colyton Grammar School or Axminster Secondary Modern. This left Axmouth as just a village primary school, and that was how it remained until its closure in the summer of 1959. Falling pupil numbers were a contributory factor in the closure of the school, as was the death of Miss Maud Sanders Stephens, Lady of the Manor at Stedcombe, who died in 1959. The pupils of the school were transferred to Seaton School after their return from the school summer holidays.

The Exeter Diocesan Board of Finance took over the building, and Mrs Judith Vanda Sanders Berry of Millmead, Axmouth, bought the building and adjoining land from the Diocesan Board in 1960. The inaugural meeting of the Village Hall Committee was held on 20 September 1961, when Mrs Berry made a gift of the Axmouth Village School and a parcel of land adjoining the churchyard to the Parish Council for the use of the public. Mrs Berry hoped the hall would become a centre in which everyone could meet and enjoy themselves for years to come.

Teachers at Axmouth School over the years included Mr Gill, Mr Borne, Mrs Major, Gwen Owen and Winifred Copp. The last two teachers at the school were Miss Phyllis Thompson and Mrs Joan Westwood.

Axmouth Pre-School (3–5 year olds) Group in the playground of Axmouth Village Hall, 27 June 2005. The staff are Sue Dare (Manager), Louise Winwood (Assistant), Roslyn Jackson (Assistant). Back row, left: Sydney Hammond, Alistair Herbert, Ellie Evans, Xavier King. Front row: Nancy McLoughlin, Eldon Hulme, Helen Underwood, Jonathan Jacks, Rebecca Smitham, William House.

Axmouth Village School infants, 1927. Back row, left to right: Victor Morgan, Peter Real, Roy Webber, George Morgan, Dick Spiller, Reg Anning, Arthur Ayres, Harry Morgan, Maurice Webber. Middle row: Margery Snell, Miriam Tipper, Ida Harvey, Ada Rice. Front row: Horace Crichard, Stella Morgan, Dorothy Morgan, Winnie Morgan, Harold Richards.

The children of Axmouth celebrating the coronation of Edward VII. The king was crowned in 1902, and the children of Axmouth were assembled at the school to have this photograph taken by George Barton, the Seaton photographer. He left behind a picture of great charm, depicting a quaint, old-fashioned group, the girls in their ankle-length frocks and white pinafores, the boys in hob-nailed boots. It must have been a memorable day for the children, whose lives were restricted by poverty and other hardships. Occasions like this were an escape from the narrow world in which they lived.

Axmouth School football team, 1933. Back row, left to right: Ben Newbery, Frank Parker, Harry Morgan, Arthur Ayres. Middle row: Clem Goodland, George Morgan, Peter Real, Roy Webber, Horace Crichard. Front row: Philip Soper, Victor Morgan.

Axmouth School infants, 1921. Back row, left to right: Ronnie Newbery, Gordon Real, Arthur Lomax, Eddie Spiller. Middle row: Mr Borne (headmaster), Edward Spiller, Jack Real, Herbert Morgan, Leslie Harvey, Arthur Tipper, 'Beck' Major (schoolmistress). Front row: Emma Morgan, Walter Newbery, Vincie Snell, Betty Spiller, Eileen Morgan, George Perry, Dick Webber, Holway Webber, -?-.

Axmouth School group, *c.* 1905.

Axmouth School football team, 1922. Back row, left to right: Fred Ayres, Oliver Perry, Joe Poole, Mick Dack, Jack Crichard, Ken Webber. Front row: Arthur Tipper, Alec Summers, Ivor Real, Tom Morgan, Ken Crichard, Herbie Morgan.

Axmouth School football team, 1932. Back row, left to right: Ben Newbery, Peter Real, Maurice Webber, Douglas Morgan. Middle row: Horace Crichard, George Morgan, Arthur Ayres, Harry Morgan (who was killed in action while serving in the Royal Navy during the Second World War). Front row: Victor Morgan, Roy Webber, Philip Soper.

Axmouth Primary School, 1953. Back row, left to right: Leslie Legg, Robin Legg, Barbara Spiller, Pauline Real, Celia Morgan, Keith Dack. Middle row: Bruce Dack, Maxwell Dack, Carole Widger, Sandra Key, Jeannie Johns, Gwen Ostler, Shirley Newbery, Tony Widger, Brian Tipper. Front row, seated: Sandy Dack, Michael Clement, Clifton Real, Ronald Real, Keith Millman, Keith Legg. Note the old servicemen's clubhouse, behind the schoolchildren. This was pulled down shortly after this photograph was taken, and Marandellas was built.

Axmouth Gospel Hall and St Michael's Church, *c.* 1948. These are the combined Sunday Schools, together with children from Seaton. They are at Seaton Congregational Church for a tea party and lantern slide show. Axmouth children (second table back from middle of photograph), left to right: Nancy Sweetland, Ann Real, Ivy Beasley, June Clement?, Lavinia Blackmore, Maureen Humphrey, Pat Dack, Ruth Newbery, Faith Griffiths, Rosemary Spiller, Mary Millman, Barbara Spiller, Celia Morgan. First full table (middle nearest camera): Bruce Dack, Robin Legg, Albert Snell, Leslie Legg, Mervyn Legg, Ross Dack, Michael Sweetland, Herbie Sweetland, Ted Humphrey, Paul Northcott, Raymond Puddicombe, John Webber, Brian Tipper, Roger Webber.

Axmouth School football team, 1937. Back row, left to right: David Newbery, Reg Larcombe, Leonard Potter, Albert Larcombe, Basil Pavey, Victor Crichard. Seated: John Sweetland, Peter Sweetland, Stanley Harvey, Grenville Morgan, Douglas Spiller. Front: Derek Ostler.

Axmouth Primary School, 1955. Back row, left to right: Carole Widger, Gwen Ostler, Jeannie Johns, Sandra Key, Shirley Newbery, Jeanette Spiller. Middle row: Maxwell Dack, Clifton Real, Janet Newbery, Pamela Walley, Carole Key, Stella Soper, Anne Newbery, Ronald Real, Tony Widger. Front row, seated: Keith Millman, Rodney Morgan, Keith Legg, Gerald Morgan, Frank Quick, Peter Charman, Frankie Beer, Michael Clement, Sandy Dack.

Axmouth Primary School, 1956. This was probably one of the last school photographs taken. When Miss Stephens, the Lady of the Manor at Stedcombe, died in 1959, the school closed. With the start of the autumn term in 1959 the children transferred to Seaton Primary School. Back row, left to right: Clifton Real, Frankie Beer, Tony Widger, Sandy Dack, Keith Millman. Middle row: Ronald Real, Keith Legg, Stella Soper, Janet Newbery, Shirley Newbery, Jeanette Spiller, Carole Widger, Carole Key, Michael Clement, Rodney Morgan. Front row, kneeling: Gerald Morgan, Ian Widger, Melvin Millman, Carol Hoare, Monica Clement, Anne Newbery, Frank Quick, Peter Wright. Front, seated: Tim Soper, Clive Millman.

Axmouth Primary School, 1949. Back row, left to right: Pauline Real, Maureen Humphrey, Jean Kaxi, Lavinia Blackmore, Pat Dack, Rosemary Spiller, Barbara Spiller. Middle row: Terry Pavey, Raymond Puddicombe, Alan Johns, Jennifer Nash, Donald Ostler, Celia Morgan, Ross Dack, Paul Northcott, Albert Snell, Mervyn Legg. Front row, kneeling: Bruce Dack, Leslie Legg, Michael Sweetland, Sandra Key, Jeannie Johns, Heather Cockram, Gwen Shepherd, Gwen Ostler, Keith Dack, Robin Legg, David Vaughan. Front row, seated: Maxwell Dack, Keith Nash, Tony Widger, Barry Clarke, Sandy Dack.

Children waiting to go to Seaton Primary School by the bus shelter, Stepps Lane, July 2005. The children were out of uniform to go on a trip along the Jurassic coast by boat from Seaton. Left to right, back row: Annabelle Woodman, Victoria Herrity, Benjamin Bastin Wood, Kate Ostler. Front row: Thomas Bastin Wood, Jess Spiller, Megan Spiller.

Children waiting to go to Seaton Primary School from Chapel Street, 1 July 2005. Back, left to right: mums Alex Smart, Sylvia Winder; front: Bryony Smart, Anna Winder, Joe Winder.

5

Stedcombe

The present-day owners of Stedcombe House, seen on the terrace, are Victoria and Christopher Rae Scott with son Philip, 5 September 2005.

Stedcombe shooting scene, c. 1880. Seen here are Robert Collins, Major Wills, Colonel Hallett, (seated) – Squire Hallett of Stedcombe Manor, Thomas Dare Chappell of Bindon, Robert Palmer, who was born on 19 January 1811, and was the first to see the devastation of the Landslip in 1839. The family of Thomas Chappell owned Bindon for many years, and his father made a great deal of money by charging visitors to view the Landslip in 1840. He died on 5 May 1902.

Maud Elizabeth Sanders Stephens, aged two, 7 July 1888. When Miss Stephens died in 1959 it signified the end of the village as many knew it. The village school closed, all the farms went, and a way of life that had revolved round the manor house disappeared. Maud Stephens is buried in the family vault in Axmouth churchyard. Miss Leech, the governess, died in March 1953, at the grand old age of ninety-one.

In the flower garden at Stedcombe, September 1900. Guy Sanders Fiske (in pram) with Maud Elizabeth Sanders Stephens, aged fourteen. Behind her is governess Florence Katherine Sinclair Leech.

The carriage awaits – the front entrance of Stedcombe, c. 1891. This photograph was sent to Victoria Rae Scott by Judith Fiske, niece of the late Maud Stephens, and was taken from the Stephens family album.

In early times Stedcombe belonged to the Uffeville and Vere families and by the fourteenth century it had become the property of the Courtenays. The manor was granted by Henry VIII to Sir Peter Carew, from whom it was purchased by Walter Yonge Esq. His descendent, Sir Walter Young Bt, sold both Stedcombe and the Manor of Axmouth to Richard Hallett Esq. Stedcombe then became a part of the Manor of Axmouth and the seat of Richard Hallett, who became the principal impropriator of the great tithes, which belonged to the Monastery of Syon.

Stedcombe Manor, Axmouth, 1904. The Lord of the Manor, Samuel Sanders Stephens, had just been made High Sheriff of Devon and the children of Axmouth village school were waiting in the driveway by Stedcombe lodge to cheer him home.

Villagers and family gather together for this picture in Stedcombe House grounds, on the occasion of the 21st birthday of Maud Elizabeth Sanders Stephens, 10 March 1907. Maud Stephens died on 13 May 1959, aged seventy-three, at Stedcombe House.

Some of the staff at Stedcombe Manor photographed in the late 1930s. Back, left to right: Len Weekes (gardener), Scobie (Jock) Hamilton (chauffeur). Front: -?- (the young lady was a chamber maid from Wales, and she died young from tuberculosis), Annie Madley (cook), Elizabeth Newbery (kitchen maid).

James Henry Parsons (coachman at Stedcombe) and Annie Madley (cook at Stedcombe), *c.* 1914.

Stedcombe Spaniel Trials, 1960/1. Left to right: Mr Du Cross (Dowlands Farm), Dr White, John Andrew Whilley, Peter Wakley, John Pike, George Hassell (gamekeeper at Stedcombe), Mr Kent.

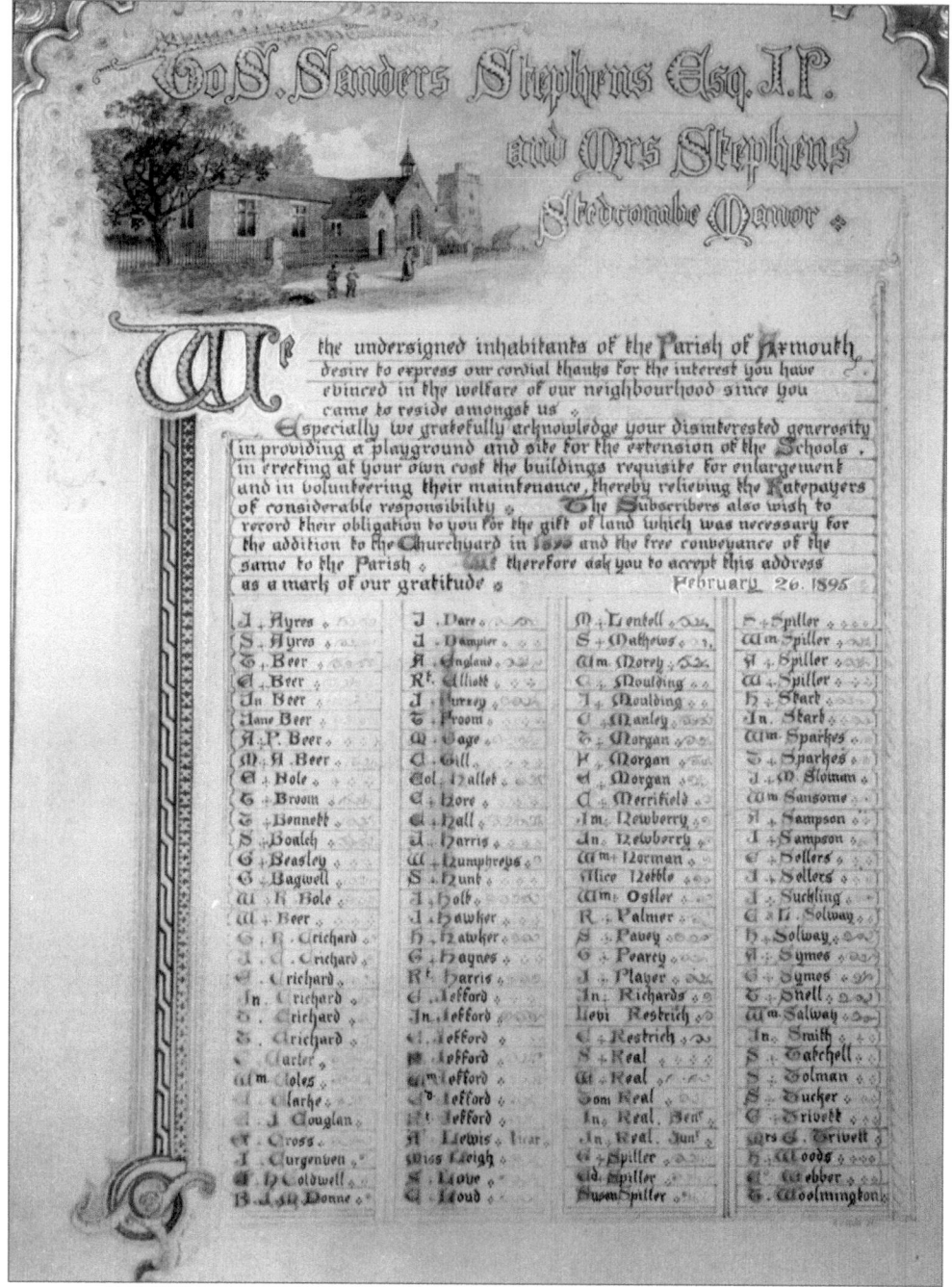

This 1895 document, now in the Village Hall, shows the undersigned inhabitants of the parish of Axmouth thanking the Lord and Lady of the Manor at Stedcombe, for providing a playground and site for an extension for the village school.

Salmon fishing on the Axe, *c.* 1931. The Axmouth residents pictured here are, from left to right, Jack Beer, Robert Dack (gamekeeper) and Maurice Webber. Keeper Dack had the rights for catching the salmon at Axe Bridge. This was done with a net and rowing boat, and on this occasion it appears the catch was just one salmon, held by Robert Dack.

Shooting party outside Stedcombe House, *c.* 1980. The photograph includes: Terry Pavey, Frank Doble, Tony Widger, Tim Dack, Bob Pavey, Phil Somers, Wally Anning, Alan Doble, Don Mariner, Mark Pavey, Gavin Foxwell, Ned Spiller, Clare Ashleigh, Bill Richards, Steve Hooper, Joe Derrick, Ken Spiller, Tim Vincent, Terry Facey, Max Dart, Peter Anning and gamekeeper Frank Betteridge (with sports jacket and tie).

Keepers Cottage, Stedcombe, 1960.

Among the most savoury of game birds, pheasants provide sport by flying strongly and directly when driven over guns. Rearing and protecting the birds, and organising shoots, is a major rural industry. In this photograph, taken in 1961, the gamekeeper of the Stedcombe Estate Shoot, George Hassell, can be seen tending his chickens, which were used for hatching pheasant eggs. The rearing pens are all stock-proofed with wire fencing to stop foxes getting in.

Church garden fête, 7 July 1955. This fête was held to raise money for changing from oil lighting to electric lighting in the Parish Church of St Michael. Back row, left to right: Ambrose Spiller, Vincent Martyn, Danny Hughes (with his wife Margery in front and two sons), Ruth Newbery, Elizabeth Gush, Joyce Harvey, Michael Gush. Front row: Mary Broom, Mr and Mrs Fred Abbot, Dora Griffiths (the vicar's wife), the Revd Hugh Peregrine Griffiths, Mrs Hudson, Miss Grey (housekeeper at Stedcombe), Mrs Eyles, Annie Madley (cook at Stedcombe).

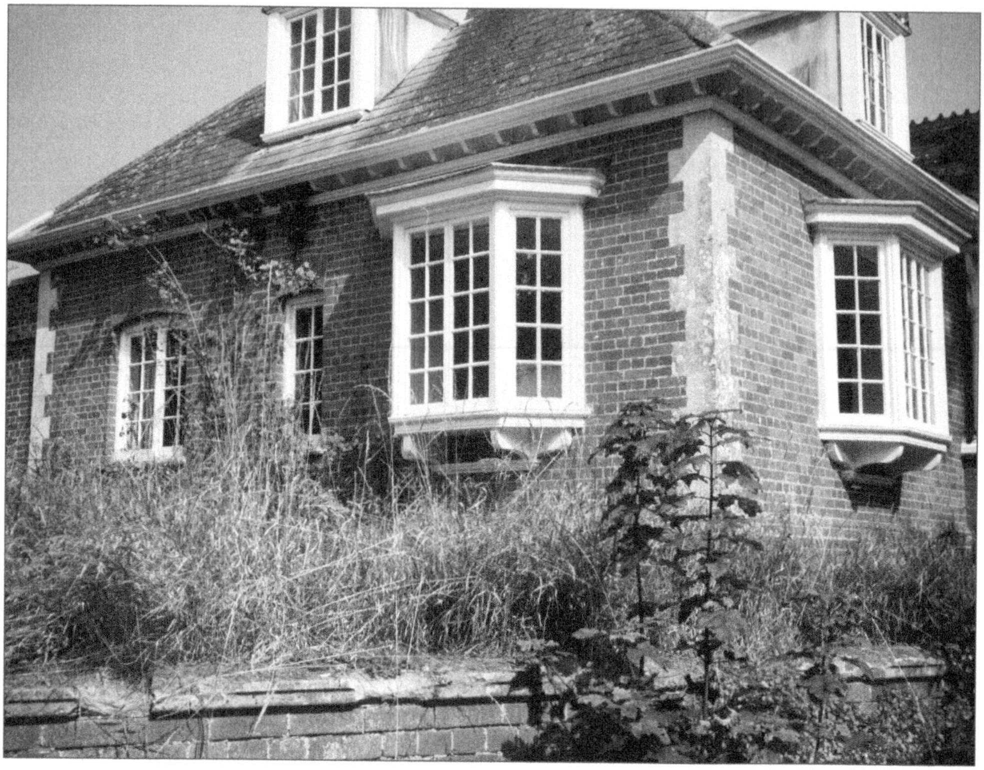

Stedcombe Lodge, *c.* 1984. The lodge is situated at the bottom of the drive from Stedcombe House. When this photograph was taken the lodge and manor house had been neglected for a number of years. Both are now occupied, and have been restored.

By order of the Executors of Miss M. E. S. Sanders Stephens

PRICE 1/-

STEDCOMBE MANOR

Axmouth, Nr. Seaton, Devon

ATTRACTIVE SALE OF

FURNITURE

29th & 30th September, 1959
at 11 a.m.

JACKSON-STOPS & STAFF
YEOVIL

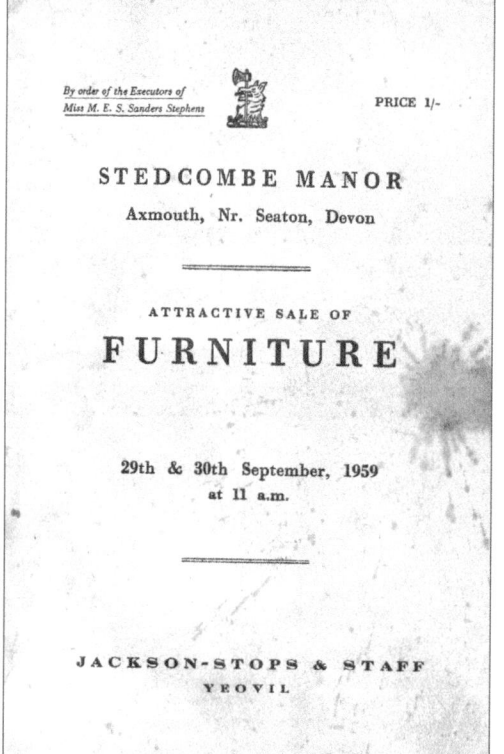

The sale catalogue of the contents of Stedcombe Manor, which was conducted over two days by Jackson-Stops of Yeovil, on 29 and 30 September 1959.

6

The Axmouth Floods

In 1960, houses in this area of Axmouth were flooded to a depth of 5ft, and this householder appears to be wondering where to start. After the flood, parties of boys from Axmouth and Seaton volunteered to help with the clear-up operation.

The worst disaster to hit East Devon in living memory came at about 2 a.m. on the morning of 1 October 1960. On this night 3in of rain cascaded down, and within minutes the centuries-old village of Axmouth, laying hard on the River Axe, was swimming in water.

Heavy rain fell in the catchment area of the small stream which runs down the centre of the village. The force of the water carried trees and boulders, which built up to form a dam, behind which a small lake formed. When the dam burst, a tidal wave of floodwater shot down the valley. The flood hit Axmouth in the small hours, but had it come at 2 p.m., cars and people would have been swept away.

Seaton police sergeant Donald Cowling received an SOS call at 3 a.m. and, with PC George Rudd, he drove to Axmouth. Sergeant Cowling told reporters later that:

> As we got near the village the road just disappeared under water. We waded up the street, which was like a river, and then an absolute torrent swept down and we had to cling to the church railings. The road was like a roaring river, and dustbins and rocks were being thrown all over the place.

Following the flood, help came from the fire brigade and the WVS, and parties of boys from Axmouth and Seaton went round asking people if they could help clear up the mess. 'I shall never run down teenagers again', said an elderly Axmouth woman, 'they have done a wonderful job.'

The stream had not flooded for the previous 100 years, and with luck it may be 100 years or more before it floods again. If similar rainfall conditions occur again, however, who knows?

This was the scene on the main road at Axmouth, where houses were flooded and tons of stones washed into the road.

The road near Coombe Orchard was in a terrible state.

Cleaning up after the flood was an arduous and unpleasant job, and many people lost virtually all their downstairs belongings. Here we see local residents bailing out water from their cottages. Unfortunately these thatched cottages were demolished at a later date, and replaced with a modern building.

For the second time in four days, over 7in of rain fell at Axmouth, and nearly 4in fell on the fateful morning, leaving scenes like this.

Anybody who has never seen the aftermath of a flood cannot possibly imagine the devastation. Here the flood-hit residents are putting out precious belongings and furniture on the street to dry.

Axmouth village the morning after the flood.

7

High Days & Events

Pictured here in October 1955 at Axmouth Gospel Hall are members of the chapel making a presentation to Doris Clement to commemorate her marriage to Charles Harris. Left to right: Dinah Millman, Laura Clement, Winifred Maidment, May Tucker (presenting the gift of a companion set), Mrs Partridge of Stedcombe Farm, Doris Clement, Mrs Hudson, Lily Spiller, Alice Larcombe.

The Axe Cliff Golf Club, with its position on the summit of Haven Cliff, commands magnificent views stretching from Portland Bill to Start Point. This is one of the earliest photographs known of the club, taken at the club house in 1904.

Viewed across over a century of war and economic crisis, the England of Edward VII appears to have been a place of peace and prosperity. This group of golfers from the Axe Cliff Golf Club, who stopped to have their photograph taken, captures the atmosphere of that brief Indian summer.

Two unique photographs showing the construction of Waterside, the new road to Seaton from Axmouth, 1924.

Empire Day celebrations, c. 1925. Before the 1930s this was a school holiday and an occasion of much rejoicing. Empire Day was held on Queen Victoria's birthday, 24 May, and originated in commemoration of the assistance given by the colonies in the Boer War, 1899–1902.

During August 1943 a week of events, including a fête at Stedcombe, raised £550 for the Red Cross. Pictured here are the winners of the children's fancy dress competition: 2–5 years age group: 1st Maureen Humphrey (Britannia), 2nd Peter Goodland (Syd Walker), 3rd Pauline Real (Queen of Hearts). 5–7 years: 1st Ann Real (Squanderbug), 2nd Teddy Humphrey (John Bull), 3rd Evelyn Clement (flower girl). 8–11 years: 1st June Sweetland (Squanderbug), 2nd Rodney, Mary and David Burridge (stretcher party), 3rd Mary Kaxi (flower girl). 11–14 years: 1st Margaret Northcott (rainbow), 2nd Amy Sweetland (Scotsgirl), 3rd Mary Hamilton (nurse). Also Ruth Newbery (nurse), Nancy Sweetland (Red Riding Hood) and Paul Northcott (Cossack). The little boy on the right is pushing a cart with the caption 'Syd Walker Any Rags or Bones'. Syd Walker is not a familiar name today, but at that time he was a leading figure on BBC radio, and had his own show. During the war years he lived in the neighbouring town of Seaton.

Devon is famous for its cider, and this old song gives a guarantee of long life to those who drink it:

> In an East Devon village not far from the sea
> Still lives my old Grandad aged ninety and three.
> Of orchards and meadows he owns a good lot
> Such as his – not another has got.
> My Grandad is lusty, is nimble and spry
> As Ribstons his cheeks, clear as crystal his eye.
> His head snowy white as the flowering May
> And he drinks only cider by night and by day.

Axmouth has a tradition that the first cider in Devon was made in the village. Whether or not this is true, the fact remains that cider presses were commonplace in the nineteenth century in nearly every farm in East Devon. Nowadays cider presses are antiques much coveted by incomers to give a period flavour to their restored country cottages. It is somehow sad to think that they lapsed from common use to become valued merely as decorations. Nevertheless, cider-making is still carried on in Axmouth and here, on 7 November 2005 in the barn opposite Stepps House, we see Nigel Daniel with a shovelful of chopped apples from the mill. He is preparing to load the 'cheese' in the cider press manned by Di Taylor and Pat Trezise. The best cider came from the Royal Wilding apple, though another good cider apple was the Midyate. The liquor made from this apple was known as bramble cider, because in swallowing it one felt a sensation as if a bramble had been thrust down one's throat and snatched back again. Lovers of really rough cider gave it preference over all other sorts. I doubt that apples from those old Victorian trees are still available today.

This photograph, taken in the barn belonging to David Trezise in Stepps Lane, shows a group of villagers assisting in the making of cider, 7 November 2005. The apples are being put through the cider mill to be chopped up. David Trezise and Jane Calvert turn the wheels of the mill, while Bill Richardson pushes down the apples. Nigel Daniel, below, shovels out the chopped apples to go into the 'cheese' of the cider press and Mike Calvert stands in the background.

The cider press in the barn at Stepps Lane.

Seaton Sea Rangers, 1958. The success of the Seaton Sea Rangers movement depended very much on the Axmouth connection. Skipper Margaret Northcott is seen here, top left. In 1949, nine years before this picture was taken, a muster took place, and many village names were listed. Skipper, Mrs T. Mayo: Number One, Miss M.E. Payne: Number Two, Miss M. West: Boatswain of Port Watch, Miss June Sweetland: Shantyman, Frances Copp: Librarian, Janet Tolman: Stewards, Margaret Northcott and Jean Snell. Crew, Starboard Watch: Margaret Northcott, Jean Snell, Barbara Newton, Jill Pallet, Rosemary Adams, Frances Copp, Sheila Marsh, Ann Pearson, Marion Powling, Ann Hammett, Ann Real. Port Watch: June Sweetland, Barbara Vaughan, Jeanette Slynn, Elsie Bryant, Margaret Gooding, Janet Tolman, Margaret Davey, June Barrett, Ruth Newbery, Nancy Sweetland, Margaret Bailey.

Seaton Carnival, c. 1948. Seaton ironmongers Frank Akerman & Co. Ltd are pictured with the tableau they entered in the carnival. In the centre is Mr Puddicombe from Axmouth, who worked for the firm for many years.

Axmouth Flower Show, c. 1955. The flower show was held behind the Harbour Inn. Left to right: Laura Clement, Mary Broom, Win Sweetland, Jim Cross, Mrs Doble, George Johns, Geoffrey Spiller, Edward Spiller, Mrs Pugh, Bob Pugh.

Square Dance Party at Stepps Guest House, c. 1955. Back row, left row right: Barbara Vaughan, Alexandra Doble, Mary Broom, Laura Clement, Mary Chard, Winifred Sweetland, Pat Metcalfe, Vice Admiral Sir Francis Pridham, Grenville Morgan, Major Russell Price, Betty Widger, Rose Real, Robin Grant. Middle row: Emma Johns, Margaret Northcott, Olive Real, Dorothy Strawbridge, Mary Webber, Lady Pridham, Alice Larcombe, Mrs Mackay Ohm, Betty Furzey, Mrs Price, Donald Hansford, -?-. Seated: Ann Real, P. Steel, Kathleen Ostler, George Johns, Nancy Sweetland, -?-, Irene Beasley, Dennis Morgan.

One of the most revolutionary changes after the First World War was the coming of the motor bus, which was then known as the charabanc. Here a party from the Axmouth Gospel Hall can be seen en route to Cheddar Caves, *c.* 1928. In such photographs the roof of the vehicle always seems to be down, and with the passengers all wearing a variety of hats, did they all stay on when the driver got his charabanc up to 20mph, or did they have to make numerous stops to retrieve lost headgear? The passengers include John Richards, Charlie Harvey, Geoffrey Spiller, Ned Spiller, Minnie Spiller, Alfred Morgan, Edith Real and Jack Real.

St Michael's Church Sunday School outing, *c.* 1954. Looking out from the bus window, left to right: Harry Newbery, Gladys Spiller, Olive Soper, Mrs Newton, the Revd Hugh Griffiths. Standing: Ruth Newbery, Phyllis Real, Mary Chown, Ethel Clement, Rosemary Spiller, Jean Sherret, Barbara Spiller, Faith Griffiths, Barry Clarke, Mrs Dora Griffiths. Front: Monica Clement, Jennifer Clarke, Pamela Walley, Anne Donaldson, Joy Walker, Stella Soper, Tim Soper, Ronald Real, Richard Gush.

Souvenir programme of the Axmouth celebrations on the occasion of the coronation of Queen Elizabeth II, Tuesday 2 June 1953.

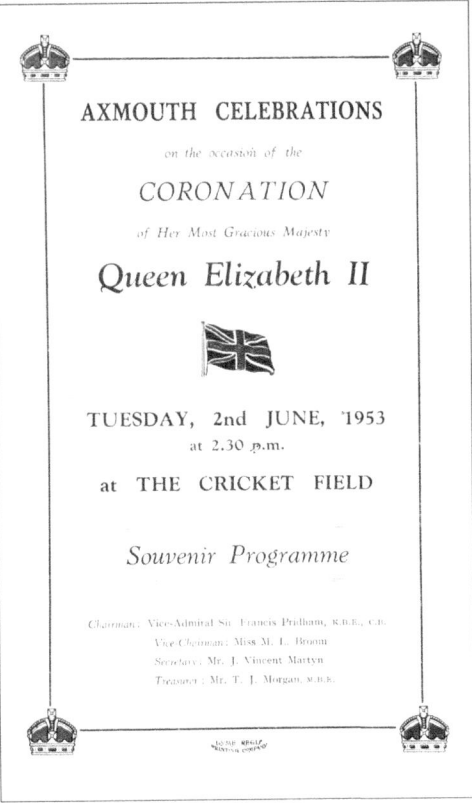

Souvenir programme of events to celebrate the Silver Jubilee of Queen Elizabeth II, 7 June 1977.

The year 1993 saw the presentation of *The Wizard of the Axe*, and some of the children in the show include Lauren Jackson, Rosie Midgley, Hannah Boalch and Ellen Maclean.

vvvvvvvvvv was the pantomime performed in 1992. Back row, left to right: the Revd Stuart Worth, David Trezise, Paul Midgley, Roger Webber and Norman Owen. Second row: Hannah Boalch, Rachel Deam, Rosie Midgley, -?-, Robert Steven, Lauren Jackson, -?-, Emma Boalch. Third row: 'The Rat' (actor unknown), Ellen Maclean, Jennie Sansom, Gemma Millman, Alice Jackson, Tim Vincent, Christopher Sansom, Charlotte Paley. Front row, seated: Terry Midgley, -?-.

The management of sheep flocks is important, and a few weeks after they are shorn they are dipped against blowflies, ticks and other parasites. Seen here are Peter Sweetland (in the foreground) and Albert Soper dipping sheep from Coombe Farm at Bindon Coombe, c. 1954. The sheep dip was built into the course of the village brook, which was dammed up with a sliding board. The sheep dip was destroyed in the flood of October 1960 and never replaced.

Mike Clement as John Bull and Sue Widger as Oliver Hardy are seen here at a New Year's Eve fancy dress party and disco at the Harbour Inn, 1987. The event, organised by Axmouth United FC, was a fund-raising event for the new ground at Boshill Cross.

During August 2004, a Flower Festival was held in St Michael's Church, organised by Christine Badger. Pictured here, with Christine Badger on the far left, are the ladies who helped to make this festival an outstanding success. Left to right: Carol Smith, Barbara Newbery, Betty Lawrey, Doris Clement, Celia Powell, Rosemary Tidball, Betty Board, Lyn White, Olive Owen, Mary Britain, Jill Tizzard, Minnie Newbery.

Keepers' and Beaters' Dinner, Pole Arms, Seaton, 1963. Standing, left to right: Michael Pidgeon, Malcolm Doble, Percy Real, Charlie Gapper, -?-, Len Key, Fred Rowland, Gerald Hazeldean, George Perry, Arthur Turner, -?-, Ira Pidgeon. Seated: George Hassell (gamekeeper at Stedcombe), gamekeeper Mr Hall (Rousdon), Mr Du Cross (Dowlands), Frank Doble.

Herbie Sweetland is pictured here in the old football field behind the Harbour Inn, with the three cups that he had won at the annual Axmouth Flower Show, c. 1963.

On 2 May 1982, in support of the Maritime Year events, the Seaton Chamber of Trade organised a boat race from Axmouth to Axmouth Bridge with competing university crews. It took place under appalling conditions, with an off-sea gale with the incoming tide. In this photograph we see crews from Bristol and Cambridge.

The Exeter crew rowing under Axmouth Bridge, 2 May 1982.

A rare sight in Axmouth Harbour, the crew from Oxford University going down to the start.

Christmas at the Harbour Inn, *c.* 1967. In the back row are David Vaughan, Terry Pavey, Keith Millman. Front: Herbie Clement, Frank Sartin.

Axmouth FC children's christmas party, held at Axmouth Village Hall, 1962. Some of the people featured in this photograph include Norma Sweetland, Nancy Sweetland, Betty Board, Laura Clement, Alice Larcombe, Linda Pike, Georgie Pidgeon, Pat Bewick, Monica Clement, Ian Widger, Clive Millman, Janet Newbery, Jennie Clarke, Richard Gush, Margery Ostler, David Ostler, Barbara Newbery, Lynn Newbery, Betty Hoare, Winifred Sweetland, David Board, Nigel Morgan, Stephen Millman and Michael Gush.

The ceremony of the burning of the ashen faggot at the Harbour Inn was broadcast by the BBC in 1950, and again for a television programme in 1952. Pictured here we have the ashen faggot in readiness for Christmas Eve 1951.

David Trezise, Mike Calvert, Brian Davis and Ian Hunt are seen here on 24 December 2005 gathering ash branches in preparation for making the Ashen Faggot. The ceremony of the Burning of the Ashen Faggot was held at the Harbour Inn on Christmas Eve. The Ashen Faggot, 6ft in length, would be tied together with seven hazel binds and taken down to the Harbour Inn on Christmas Eve morning ready for the evening ceremony.

Christine and Ron Badger are seen here cooking breakfast in the campsite field, summer 2004. This event was held to raise funds for repairs to St Michael's Church.

Owl Night at the Ship Inn, held in aid of Newbury Wildlife Hospital, November 1978. Landlady Jane Chapman, on the right, presents a cheque to the owners of the hospital after a fundraising event.

Axmouth Football Club boules team of the Axe Valley Boules League, Division 1. On this occasion they were playing the Golden Hind 'A' from Musbury, 28 June 2005. Back row, left to right: Steve Cross, Denise Cross, Sue Gush, Pat Cooper, Rodney Gush. Front: Mike Clement, Doris Clement.

A fund-raising event organised by Allhallows School and Axmouth United FC was held in the summer of 1990. The event was held at Allhallows to raise money for the football club, which had just bought its new ground at Musbury. Ten brave ladies were sponsored to abseil down the school clocktower (the tall building in the background). Back, left to right: Doris Clement, Delia Park, Barbara Dorward, Michelle Wood, Julie McArthur, Susan Dack. Front: -?-, Frances Northcott, Glenda Board, Olive Real.

The value of trees to the environment was recognised in the 1947 Town and Country Planning Acts. It was decided that tree-planting and preservation should be considered in all plans for future development. The value of tree-planting is being shown to these young Axmouth boys by Aiden Winder, and under his guidance they are planting ash and oak trees at the Musbury Road football ground in 1990. Left to right: Aiden Winder, Chris French, Tristram Snell, Mark Widger, Tim Vincent, Ben Midgley and Damien Snell.

A notable date in the calendar is 5 November, Bonfire Night. This picture, taken in late October 1987 in Roger Webber's field under Hawkesdown, shows four young boys helping to build the Axmouth Football Club bonfire in preparation for the big night. Left to right: Kevin Davis, Jamie Page, Michael Davis, Matthew Page.

The wedding ceremony of Susan Widger and Neil Smart took place at St Michael's, the Parish Church of Axmouth, on 29 July 1995. Vincent Trevett can be seen in the front of this photograph, holding a bouquet, and Douglas Trevett leans over a tombstone talking to the bridegroom, who was serving with the Royal Navy.

The children seen in this photograph took part in the *Cinderella* pantomime which was put on in 1999. Back row, left to right: Jennie Sansom, Donna Billings, Jessemy Caines, Simon Goryl, Gemma Millman, Samantha Goryl. Front row: Michael Cullum, Victoria Paley, Charlotte Paley.

Axmouth Flower Show in the field behind the Harbour Inn, August 1948. In the background is Hedley Clement's coal lorry, decorated with bunting. The Allotment Association, later to become the Village Produce Association, organised the young ladies of the village into raising funds by selling penny tickets around the district, the winner becoming the Axmouth Flower Show Queen. The young ladies in the photograph are, left to right from the back: June Sweetland, Kathy Ostler, Ruth Newbery, Ivy Beasley and Irene Beasley. The young lady who sold the most tickets was Ivy Beasley, who was crowned the Flower Show Queen, with the two runners-up as attendants.

The Sunday coach trips for village folk which Miriam Legg organised during the 1950s and '60s were well supported. Here are some members of a group visiting Lynmouth in 1956. Left to right: May Tucker, Brian Tipper, Winifred Sweetland, Maureen Humphrey and Ross Dack.

In 1961 Mrs Judith Berry made a gift of the old Village School to the Parish Council for the use of the village. Here, in April 1963, Judith Berry holds her bouquet after presenting Miss Mary Broom with a commemorative plaque. Others in the picture include Donald Baker, Edith Collins, Arthur Collins, Peter Charman, Clive Millman, Gerald Morgan, Janet Newbery, Monica Clement, Richard Gush, Frank Quick, Maureen Humphrey, Lyn Newbery, Florence Clement, Joan Webber and Ken Webber.

The flooding of Axmouth post office, mid-1950s. The shop was then called Belle Vue, and was owned and run by Ambrose and Sheila Spiller. Today it is called Stone Cottage. All hands to the pumps, as one might say, for the clean up. Left to right: Phyllis Thompson (village school headmistress), Alice Larcombe, Irene Beasley and Mildred Beasley.

A happy group of holidaymakers pose for this photograph in the garden of Landslip Cottage on a hot summer's day, c. 1932.

Albert and Rose England took over Landslip Cottage some time before 1914 and continued with the tea room originally set up by the Gapper family. The menu at the time was tea, bread and butter with cake for 8d. Jam and clotted cream were 4d extra. At a later date the Gapper family moved back again. In this photograph we see members of the England family listening to their father playing the violin, c. 1913. Left to right: Beatrice, Albert (father), Maud, Rose (mother), Ethel and Elizabeth.

8

The River Axe & the Harbour

This historic photograph was taken in 1859 and shows the training wall built at the beginning of the nineteenth century by John Hallett, Lord of the Manor of Axmouth. This increased the rate of flow of the river, and helped to clear the mouth of pebbles.

Looking up the River Axe, August 1877. In this rare and important photograph the long exposure has given the water a wonderful, unearthly texture, at once blurred and milky. Twenty years before this picture was taken the estuary was busy, two schooners plying regularly between Axmouth and London. Many other vessels brought in coal and lime, but within a short time of the single railway line reaching Seaton in 1868, the River Axe closed to commercial shipping.

Axmouth was part of the past of Seaton and it comprised a sheet of water half a mile wide and 4½ miles long to Whitford. Besides Axmouth, there were ports at Seaton and Colyford. In early times it was one of the most important harbours in the west of England, and certainly one of the safest anchorages. It was protected by the Iron Age hillforts of Hawkesdown and Musbury, both situated on the boundary between the ancient tribes of the Dumnonii and the Durotriges. The Phoenicians sailed into the River Axe and established a trading post. Ancient roadways led to the harbour along three main routes from the Dartmoor, Exmoor and Taunton areas. Tin, copper, silver, lead, iron from the Mendips, wool from the Cotswolds, hides and lime were all brought in panniers by animals along these ancient roadways.

The River Axe and Seaton, *c.* 1890. Photographs like this, which show views of streets and houses that are profoundly altered, prove how quickly and immensely things change. The Seaton railway in its glory days can be seen, with blocks of Beer stone awaiting transport. The bridge over the Axe was then only thirteen years old, and you can clearly see the toll gate.

The Old Ferry, River Axe, August 1877. This remarkable photograph was taken four months after the opening of the concrete bridge over the River Axe. Before the new bridge was opened, travellers to and from Axmouth had to cross in a ferry boat, which in later years was worked by an overhead cable system. The ferryman lived in the first small house on the left, next to the warehouse. At the mouth of the river the old Custom House can be seen. This building was washed away during the gales of January 1915.

Axmouth Harbour, c. 1890.

Axmouth Harbour, *c.* 1880. With the shipping trade at an end, the harbour looks deserted, and a solitary abandoned winch is a sad reminder of a time when things were so different.

Axe Bridge, *c.* 1950. The house in the background, named Haven Cliff, was once the residence of Colonel Hallett. He was descended from John Hallett, Lord of Axmouth Manor, and during his lifetime he was a familiar sight driving a four-in-hand.

Shipping in Axmouth Harbour, c. 1860. The house on the left belonged to the ferryman. The harbour warehouses stand on the right. These were used to store goods brought into the river by vessels such as those seen here. The rates of tonnage that applied then meant that every ship carrying 10 tons or more paid the sum of 2*d* per ton. The schedule of cargo charges included items like 'cider per hogshead – 8*d*'.

Axmouth Harbour, c. 1924. This was a more peaceful place at this time, but the view remains much the same today.

The Axmouth Coastguard Watch House, which stood at the sea end of Trevelyan Road, c. 1865.

The mouth of the River Axe, showing the warehouse and the Custom House, c. 1895.

Severe flooding of the River Axe, 1973. The man on the left is Alan White, standing next to the chalet where he had lived for eleven years. Alan White was born in Beer, the son of John White, the well-known local artist. He joined the Devon Police in 1923, and was a sergeant when he retired in 1948. Mr White died in 1979, aged seventy-seven.

The River Axe, 13 October 1972. At one time the Axe had a much wider estuary, and the village of Axmouth, seen in the background, was a place of considerable importance, possessing no less than fourteen inns. Salt was panned in the surrounding marshes, and many attempts have been made over the centuries to repair the haven. Today it is a unique, subtle and very vulnerable landscape, a part of our heritage which should not be destroyed through development. If this happens, the loss of wildlife and landscape will be irreplaceable.

Axmouth Harbour in the snow, 1977.

A winter's day in early February 1978, with the road and fields along Waterside covered with snow.

This picture of Axmouth Bridge was taken in August 1877, just after the bridge was built.

Construction of the new bridge and associated roadworks was carried out by Dean & Dyball Ltd, and work started in May 1989. The scheme was designed and supervised by Devon County Council engineering department under the direction of M.R. Hawkins OBE, at a total cost of £1,912,000. On 12 October 1990 the new bridge was officially opened by Cllr Lt-Col A.J.M. Drake at a ceremony attended by the full body of councillors from Axmouth Parish Council. In 1988/9 the old bridge was strengthened and refurbished at a cost of £250,000 and will in future be used by pedestrians. In this way a remarkable old structure will be preserved for future generations to enjoy.

Axe Yacht Club members, *c.* 1950.

An aerial view of Axmouth, the River Axe and the Harbour, also including the village of Colyford, c. 1980.

Still trading under the name of the late Harold Mears, the boatyard is now owned by his son, Paul. Pictured here at the yard are, from left to right: Alex Mears (Harold's grandson), Paul Mears, Carl Beckett, Tony Heal, Kim Aplin, Bob Aplin, Alan Abbot, Roger Webber and Rex the collie.

Harold Mears' boatbuilders yard, 1961. Left to right: Roger (Sam) Searle, Tim Dack, Clive Lee and Paul Mears.

The boat seen here in 2005 in Harold Mears' boatyard was based on a Mitchell 23 and was built for Cleeves Palmer, a partner in Palmers Brewery at Bridport. The boat, Muerrena, was named after the skiing resort of Muerren, which Cleeves often visited. It had a 100 h.p. Yamaha diesel engine, and was built of fibreglass and fitted out with teak. The boat was built by Paul and Alex Mears.

Those who carve a precarious living out of the sea need boats, and many of the boats used by local fishermen were made at Harold Mears' workshop. The late Harold Mears originally came from Exmouth to start his boatyard in 1958, and the business today is still going strong under his son, Paul. The boat seen here near completion in March 1985 is a Potter, and was built by Paul Mears for Dick Davey, who would use it to lay crab-pots off Budleigh Salterton beach.

Harold Mears, who founded the boatyard on the River Axe in 1958, is pictured here in 1983, hand on the tiller, with his son Paul.

A busy scene on the River Axe, 31 July 1948.

A photograph of Beer luggers racing on the River Axe on a full evening tide, 2004. Sailing over from Beer, the luggers had to either lower their sails and mast, or not put them up at all, until they had cleared Axmouth Bridge.

A fine photograph showing the Harbour and the old Ferry House, *c.* 1960.

Axe Yacht Club prize-giving at the Bay Hotel, Seaton, 1972. Seen here are Pom Pomeroy, Robert Riethal, Bubbles Anning, Dennis Poulton, Irene Drew, Norman Anning, Lorraine Kiss, David Mettam, Ron Harwood, Andrew Kiss, Stephen Daniel, Anne Burnand, Nigel Daniel, Alan Goodman, Frank Kiss, Jack Daniel and Walter Hall.

On 2 December 1978 the fishing trawler *Fairway* came ashore and was wrecked south-east of Culverhole Point, near Corbin Rocks, Axmouth. Several attempts were made to salvage her, but without success, and in the end she was blown up. This photograph was taken in the early summer of 1979, and shows the wreck of the *Fairway* lying among the rocks. In the background is the digger used to try to salvage the trawler. This, too, was left on the beach, to be smashed up by heavy seas over the years.

This photograph shows the Guernsey-registered fishing vessel Fairway high and dry on the rocks, just east of Culverhole Point, December 1978. The trawler was declared a complete wreck, and although attempts were made to salvage the vessel, eventually it was blown up and completely lost.

The widespread flooding of the River Coly on 1 October 1960 caused many problems in Colyton, which can be seen in these two photographs. The flooding of the River Coly also contributed to the Axmouth floods.

These two photographs show the inundated area at nearby Colyton when the Coly burst its banks on 1 October 1960.

Landslip view, *c.* 1895. The most remarkable phenomenon of the 1839 slip was that a huge block, three-quarters of a mile long, over a quarter of a mile wide and 150ft high, slipped down about 100ft, moved seaward from the cliff it had been part of, and remained upright. This left a great chasm between the block and the inland cliff. What was now the top of this block had been part of fields, sown with wheat and turnips, and on 25 August 1840 the crop was harvested. It was a great celebration, and local girls dressed as nymphs of Ceres. These 'mountain goats' needed ropes and ladders to reach the top – hence the name Goat Island. The newspapers of the day say there were more than 10,000 spectators on the inland cliff top.

In 1955 the undercliff was declared a national nature reserve. It had been acquired as such by the Nature Conservancy, which was replaced a few years later by the Nature Conservancy Council. It extends from Devonshire Head in the east to about the middle of Axmouth Harbour in the west. The category designation 'National' confuses some. Local people, who had happily trespassed on various parts of it all their lives, thought it was acquired for the nation as a public open space, and this notion is hard to dispel. With the steady and accelerating disappearance of wild Britain, it was also a cause for celebration. The reasons for its being a nature reserve are its geology, its instability, its self-sown plant regeneration (it has the largest spontaneous ash forest known) and its favourable situation for plants, migrating birds and butterflies.

Visitors to the Landslip, *c.* 1920. These people were members of a local genteel family, the Heads from Seaton. It must have been a day when the sun was blazing in the sky and, although the ladies were in summer attire, W.H. Head Esq., the family patriarch standing on the left, was dressed in the formal manner then required.

Visitors in full Edwardian splendour pose for this picture at the Landslip, *c.* 1903. These were members of the Harman-Young family, who at that time spent their annual holiday at Seaton.

Landslip Cottage, *c.* 1920. Refreshments for visitors to the Landslip were provided at this cottage. It was said to have been built from the materials of one of the two cottages that were damaged in the slip of 1837. During the Second World War the cottage was used by the Home Guard.

Mr and Mrs Gapper, who lived at Landslip Cottage, *c.* 1933. Members of the older generation still recall with delight the walk to the Landslip and the splendid cream teas and old-fashioned hospitality shown by the Gapper family.

The old footpath going to the Undercliff, c. 1935.

The River Axe showing the old Ferry House and the Warehouse, 1960.

The Wreck of the *Berar*, 1896

The Berar was an Italian three-masted barque, which ran ashore on the rocks near Rousdon. No loss of life occurred, but the crew suffered terrible hardships and privations. A fine new iron vessel, it was smashed to pieces during the first week of October 1896.

The south of England was swept by a succession of heavy gales which did a great deal of damage on land and wreaked much havoc on the sea coast. The *Berar* was on her way from Finland to Spain, laden with about 1,200 tons of planking. In tacking from the Casquets, off the coast of France, to Start Point in the face of strong westerly gales, the Captain unsuccessfully attempted to make for Portland. The weather worsened, and the gales increased in force, so that the vessel could only be sailed under close-reefed topsails and staysails. It was then that the Captain must have lost his bearings, for on Tuesday the vessel was seen beating about hopelessly in the bay. When darkness came on, the crew heard the roar of the breakers on the shore. In spite of the effort made to bring the vessel round, the force of the wind and waves drove her broadside on the rocks, about two hundred yards on the Axmouth side of the Rousdon boundary.

The jagged rocks soon tore her plates asunder, and she quickly filled with water. The crew consisted of Captain Bertolotto, thirteen men, and two boys and nearly the whole crew was of Italian nationality. When the vessel struck the rocks most of the crew took to the rigging. On a wild wretched night and in a spot of sheer desolation, no one but the poor fellows on board had any knowledge of the disaster.

When the tide had receded, the crew scrambled over the sides and managed to reach dry land and safety.

Coastguard Duckham, attached to the Whitlands station, was the first to discover that the wreck had happened. He was on night duty and, in patrolling near the eastern end of Charton Bay, he saw what he thought seemed dim lights and heard faint sounds of voices. A closer but still cursory examination disclosed a ship on the rocks, but as yet he saw no men. He at once returned to the Whitlands coastguard station, and apprised chief boatman James Pride of the occurrence, with the result that the rest of the coastguard crew were called out to assist.

When near the spot, a blue light was burnt, the boatmen were sent off searching, and the signal rocket apparatus was requisitioned. When they reached the scene, one of the crew was encountered, but nothing could be gleaned from him as he could speak no English. At about 2.30 a.m. four members of the crew were met on the beach, in the course of the search, and they were taken to the coastguard station, nearly a mile away. In the meantime the inhabitants of the four houses in the coastguard station had been informed there was a wreck, so that by the time the four men reached, the station fires and refreshments were awaiting them. The search was continued, and in the course of a few hours all the remaining members of the crew were discovered. Assistance was given by five men from the Axmouth coastguard station, who had been called by message to the scene.

The crew were in a half-naked condition, the attire of one consisting of an oil-skin coat. The captain was found on the beach in a dazed condition, and he had to be literally carried to Whitlands. Only the captain could speak or understand a word of English. One of the lads, aged about fourteen, was in an exhausted condition, the other lad was also in a bad state when found.

About 7 a.m. on Wednesday morning Mr F. Greenham, steward to Sir Henry Peek, placed at their disposal a farm wagon in which the sailors were conveyed to Lyme Regis. They were handed over to the care of Mr W.R. Rugg, the local representative of the Shipwrecked Fishermen and Mariners' Royal Benevolent Society, who had previously been informed of the wreck.

Mr Rugg at once took them to the coffee tavern, where Mr H. Long provided them with a substantial breakfast. After the meal a return was made by the sailors to the wreck, with the object of saving what they could of their personal effects.

Eight of the men were able to recover a considerable portion of their belongings – mostly clothing. However, the remainder had left their goods and chattels on the port side of the barque, which was full of water, therefore they were irrecoverable. The men were again brought to Lyme Regis in a conveyance hired by Mr Rugg, and were given a hot meal. The eight unfortunates who had lost all their clothing were taken to Mr H. Lane's and rigged up in necessary attire, at the expense of the Shipwrecked Mariners' Society. On Wednesday Mr Butt, acting Italian Vice-Consul at Weymouth, visited Lyme Regis and interviewed the men, also making arrangements for their future movements. The crew slept at the Dolphin Inn for the night, and after breakfast on Thursday morning were conveyed to Axminster railway station whence they proceeded to London by means of passes issued by the Mariners' Society.

It was at first thought that with luck the vessel might be got off the rocks and again made seaworthy. This hope was rudely dispelled two days after the vessel came ashore, when a rough sea again set in, the masts went over the sides of the ship and shortly afterwards the vessel split in two. Photographs showed the heavy wrought ironwork like stays and decking being bent about like paper.

Salvage operations immediately commenced, and the whole of the cargo and fragments of the vessel that could be saved were submitted to the hammer.

Taken from a Seaton and District Guide of 1908.

The *Berar* on the rocks, October 1896.

The *Berar* torn asunder.

ACKNOWLEDGEMENTS

Many thanks must go to those wonderful Axmouth people who gave time to talk about their native village, contributing valuable information towards the compilation of this book.

We are grateful to all those people, far too many to mention, who have loaned and given photographs and helped make the task of putting this book together a real pleasure.

Our thanks must also go to the Axmouth Village Hall Committee, Axmouth United FC, Axmouth Pre-School, the Axe Yacht Club, the Axmouth Parochial Church Council and the Devon Record Office at Exeter for allowing us to use much needed information. A special thank you goes to Judith Fiske, to Christopher and Victoria Rae Scott, and to the late Sir John and Lady Loveridge for their support.

Many books were consulted, again too many to mention, but thanks must go to Pulmans newspaper and to the *Express & Echo* for allowing us to use material from their archives. Our thanks also to Roy Chapple for writing the foreword.

We are also grateful to our wives Doris and Carol for their encouragement, and to Lyn Marshall for her assistance in the compilation of the book. Many of the old photographs in this book are truly fascinating. They bring back so vividly times past, and to live in them is never to die.